THE
QUEST FOR
PARADISE

THE
QUEST FOR
PARADISE

VISIONS OF HEAVEN AND ETERNITY IN THE WORLD'S MYTHS AND RELIGIONS

John Ashton and Tom Whyte

Harper
SanFrancisco

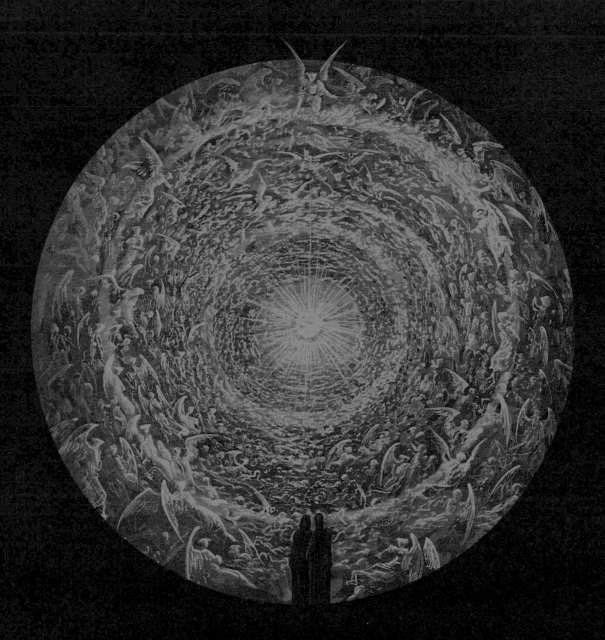

First HarperCollins Edition Published 2001

HarperSanFrancisco
A Division of HarperCollinsPublishers, Inc.
10 East 53rd Street, New York, NY 10022

HarperCollins Web site: http://www.harpercollins.com

Library of Congress Cataloguing-in-Publication Data
available upon request.

ISBN 0-06-251735-X

QUAR.NON

Conceived, designed, and produced by
Quarto Publishing plc
The Old Brewery
6 Blundell Street
London N7 9BH

Project Editors Tracie Lee Davis, Stephanie Diamond Brown
Senior Art Editor Elizabeth Healey
Designer James Lawrence
Editor Gillian Kemp
Proofreader Deirdre Clark
Indexer Dorothy Frame

Art Director Moira Clinch
Publisher Piers Spence

Manufactured by Regent Publishing Services Ltd,

Hong Kong

Printed by Star Standard, Singapore

10 9 8 7 6 5 4 3 2 1

CONTENTS

THE LONGING FOR HAPPINESS THAT IS PART AND PARCEL OF
WHAT IT MEANS TO BE HUMAN COMES TO EXPRESSION IN MANY
DIFFERENT WAYS, CHANGING ITS SHAPE FROM ONE SOCIETY TO ANOTHER.
IN THE WESTERN WORLD, FOR REASONS THAT WILL BE EXPLAINED, IT
FREQUENTLY TAKES THE FORM OF THE "QUEST FOR PARADISE" THAT GIVES
THIS BOOK ITS TITLE. ELSEWHERE IT MAY APPEAR SIMPLY AS A SEARCH
FOR IMMORTALITY OR AS AN ATTEMPT TO ATTAIN A CONDITION OF
STILLNESS AND HARMONY.

INTRODUCTION

OPPOSITE: This picture, from a 15th-century French Book of Hours, captures the moment of entry into paradise—souls about to step out of the hammock in which they have been carried up to heaven into the welcoming arms of God.

All these manifestations of the profoundly rooted human desire for happiness will be illustrated here. In the sixteenth century a new word was coined, one that was often substituted for paradise: utopia. Utopias too will have their place in the pages that follow.

In the first of the three large sections into which this book is divided, "Immortal Longings," both the word "paradise" and the garden of delights to which it refers are missing. The desire for happiness that, as Aristotle saw, characterizes humanity itself, does not always involve the use of the imagination to picture an ideal place. To suppose that it does is a common misconception, and the very first chapter, which is devoted to Ancient Sumer, the oldest civilization known to us, is partly designed to guard against this erroneous view. Still, many societies do have the concept of a blissful resting place, temporary or permanent as the case may be, and this part of the book, which mostly deals with past civilizations, but also investigates the Eastern traditions of Buddhism and Hinduism, illustrates some of these.

"The Eden Story," the second and central section of the book, is concerned with paradise in the proper sense of the word: a garden of delights. This is a concept shared by the three great monotheistic religions, Judaism, Christianity, and Islam, though it too is subject to variation and its true origin is often veiled. Two broad strands may be distinguished. In the first, which begins with the Garden of Eden itself, paradise is still situated on earth, and accordingly the quest for paradise was sometimes conceived quite literally as a conscious attempt to rediscover the original site of the garden (always believed to be far away to the east). Imagined as still existing somewhere on earth, paradise appears in many other guises too, ranging from the monastic cloister, with the opportunities it affords of quiet contemplation, to the oddly named "Land of Cockaigne," where the delights on offer are very earthy indeed.

Alternatively, paradise came to be transported by the religious imagination high up into the sky, and thus became synonymous with heaven, as it is, for instance, in

Dante's Paradiso. (In many European languages the word for sky and the word for heaven are the same: French *ciel*—or *cieux*, Italian *cielo*.) The change of place is accompanied by a radical shift of focus: up in the sky, paradise is still an object of earnest longing, but the longing is now directed forward into an imagined future, not backward into a long-vanished past. The emotion the word evokes is no longer one of wry regret but of wistful expectation, sometimes quite robust, sometimes feeble, depending upon the strength of a person's faith. All three of the great religions, though in very different ways, include a heavenly paradise in their mystical traditions.

In the third part of the book, "Other Worlds," the story is carried forward to the present day and beyond, as spiritual concepts of paradise and secular concepts of utopia are explored. The shift of focus that accompanied the move from an earthly to a heavenly paradise is mirrored in the use of this relatively new word utopia, for though some utopias are still located in the past, they are more often pictured as ideally perfect worlds realizable, if at all, only in a far distant future. Such utopias as belong to the present are fleeting, evanescent.

African, Rastafarian, and Aboriginal religions are different: even the word "paradise" often needs to be applied with caution, since in some parts of the world it resonates with the proselytizing efforts of missionaries and the colonial era. The themes of Eden (and where appropriate the Genesis story itself) are examined in relation to the power of Nature, which is often seen as being synonymous with the idea of the supreme being. In the western world, the biblical story of Eden has strongly influenced the evolution of the "American Dream" and the idea that the land is—or can be—a paradise, and this is explored within the terms of American literature. The book concludes with a brief exploration of the scientific and spiritual concept of Gaia, showing that contemporary ecological debates have extended the traditional boundaries of the Garden of Eden by placing the garden in a global context.

The human race has discovered a myriad ways of representing its elusive goal of lasting happiness.

But as the following pages demonstrate, all of these, however colorful, however mysterious, are imbued with the same sense of intangible and ineradicable longing.

LEFT: A wooden statue of Tutankhamun, from his tomb in Egypt, c.1350 B.C.E. The statue provided the deceased with a body for his spirit to occupy and thus ensured the deceased's successful journey to the sun. The statue is painted black to give it life.

OPPOSITE: A Tibetan Buddhist depiction of the Wheel of Life, detailing the cycle of rebirth and the different realms of existence. Yama, the Lord of Death, holds the Wheel in his mouth, showing that all beings live in the "jaws of death."

In the central circle, a pig, rooster, and snake represent ignorance, greed, and hatred, respectively. The black and white inner circle shows the paths of darkness and of light. The largest circle shows different states of existence. Paradise is at the top of this circle in the realm of the gods, a temporary state of being. The Buddha plays a lute to show the transitory nature of paradise.

The outermost ring shows the chain of cause and effect. In the top right, outside the wheel, the Buddha points toward enlightenment.

IMMORTAL

"GIVE ME MY ROBE; PUT ON MY
CROWN," COMMANDS SHAKESPEARE'S
CLEOPATRA AS SHE PREPARES FOR
DEATH, "I HAVE IMMORTAL LONGINGS
IN ME"—LONGINGS SHARED BY THE
MAJORITY OF THE HUMAN RACE.
ALONGSIDE THE VERY SPECIFIC
CONCEPTIONS OF PARADISE IN
THE THREE GREAT "RELIGIONS OF
THE BOOK"—JUDAISM, CHRISTIANITY,
ISLAM—MUST BE SET A MULTIPLICITY
OF VIEWS ABOUT THE AFTERLIFE IN
MANY OTHER ANCIENT CIVILIZATIONS,
INCLUDING CLEOPATRA'S EGYPT. ALL
OF THEM, HOWEVER STRANGE AND
VARIED THEIR BELIEFS, WERE
RELUCTANT TO ENTERTAIN THE
POSSIBILITY OF TOTAL EXTINCTION.

LONGINGS

THE LIVING DEAD

THE OPPOSITES OF DAY AND NIGHT, LIGHT AND DARK, ARE IMPORTANT MOTIFS WITHIN EARLY RELIGIONS. WHILE THE SUMERIANS EXPECTED TO ENDURE ETERNITY IN THE GLOOM OF THE HOUSE OF DUST, THE ANCIENT EGYPTIANS ENVISAGED A BRIGHTER FUTURE, LINKING THE AFTERLIFE TO THE SUN.

The Ancient Egyptians and the Aztecs both worshipped the sun. Just as the sun crossed the sky each day, so a content soul could enjoy the possibilities of an idyllic afterlife living within the sun or enjoying a separate paradise. The night, though, was threatening, for it symbolized the dark and dismal prospect of an existence in the underworld.

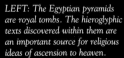

LEFT: *The Egyptian pyramids are royal tombs. The hieroglyphic texts discovered within them are an important source for religious ideas of ascension to heaven.*

The earliest tale ever told of the never-ending human quest for paradise comes from the most ancient of the world's civilizations, that of Sumer, which flourished in Mesopotamia, modern Iraq, as far back as the fourth millennium B.C.E. It is the final part of The Epic of Gilgamesh, which tells of one man's fruitless quest for immortality. Paradise, in this conception, is not a place but the state of deathlessness. Gilgamesh could not bear the thought of his own transience. Not everything is transient— everywhere we look we see the powers of nature, powers that manifest themselves unceasingly and will last for ever. Mighty and enduring, they were thought of as divine. Being divine, gods, they did not die, unlike humans, who are mortal, and do.

THE DAWN OF HUMAN HISTORY

ENKI AND NINHURSAGA

Like all other societies the Sumerians were curious about origins, their own and that of the universe they inhabited. Their myths indicate a belief in a world shaped by the gods, who eventually created mankind to help them out in the laborious task of tilling the earth. But long before that became necessary, the gods had been actively present, organizing the universe for their own purposes. One of the myths telling this story is *Enki and Ninhursaga*, which recounts the founding of a city. Enki was the god of the fresh water that flows under the earth; Ninhursaga his reluctant consort.

The city in question is Dilmun, modern Bahrain. The discovery of numerous links between the early Mesopotamian myths and Old Testament stories such as the Flood and Noah's Ark persuaded some scholars to identify Dilmun with the Garden of Eden and consequently to see the Sumerian Dilmun as a kind of paradise. But the Eden paradise was specifically designed for human habitation, whereas Dilmun, long before the creation of mankind, belonged exclusively to the gods. So it cannot be inferred from the story that paradise was forfeited as a consequence of human disobedience. According to the myth, before becoming a city Dilmun was "virginal," "pure," "pristine": "In Dilmun the raven was not yet cawing, the partridge not cackling. The lion did not slay, the wolf did not carry off lambs, the pig had not yet learned that grain was to be eaten." There was no disease, not even headaches—and no old age. Such a description may well remind us of paradise, but this can only be because Dilmun itself was not yet really a place at all: if the lion did not kill it was

because there were no lions, if the partridge did not cackle it was because there were no partridges, and the absence of disease, senility, and death simply meant the absence of mankind.

With Dilmun still in this primitive condition the god Enki persuaded Ninhursaga to have intercourse with him. After she had given birth to a daughter Enki set off on a career of serial incest: in a succession of perfunctory copulations he deprived his daughter, his daughter's daughter, and her daughter too of their virginity. For paradise-watchers the lesson can only be that the price of civilization as we know it is the loss of all that is pristine, pure, and virginal. The behavior of Enki (as an incestuous child-abuser) reinforces the point, brutally and effectively. His sexual prowess eventually resulted in a world enriched by plants and peopled by other deities, including Ensag, the eventual lord of Dilmun. There may have been a kind of notional paradise—a utopia—before this, but it was a utopia in the original sense of a non-place. Unlike the Garden of Eden (with which it was later— mistakenly—identified) the original Dilmun never figured as an object of nostalgic longing. The myth concludes with a paean of praise for the god Enki.

GILGAMESH

Although Gilgamesh, king of Uruk, had a goddess for a mother and was himself regarded as partly divine, his is a human story, and so is its moral. Gilgamesh typifies much of humanity in being both arrogant and brave. His companion Enkidu is shocked to see him exercise the *droit du seigneur* over his subjects; but when they set off together to overcome the ogre Humbaba, they both

exhibit unusual courage. The turning-point of the story is the death of Enkidu. The preceding night he recounted to Gilgamesh a dreadful dream about the fate that awaited him in the world below. Listening to this, Gilgamesh determined to do what he could to avoid the same fate, and sought advice from the wise Uta-napishti who, like the biblical Noah (whose story was doubtless modeled on his) had survived the Flood and been granted immortality by the gods. Gilgamesh, having been set the preliminary task of keeping sleep at bay, failed dismally and slept for a week.

Soon afterward he lost his one chance of rejuvenation when the plant he had named Old Man Grown Young was stolen from him by a snake. This was the closest he ever got to achieving immortality, and eventually he was forced to confront his own death. Yet he survived death in three ways. First, and most ironically, he became Lord of the Underworld. Secondly, he left behind him as a memorial the great walls of Uruk, and the celebration of the city's feasts. Finally, in the words of an ancient Sumerian tablet that records his death, "Men, as many as are given names. . . how their names will be pronounced will never be forgotten." In fact the pronunciation of Bilgames (his Sumerian name) and Gilgamesh (his Akkadian name) was forgotten for more than three millennia. Early in the nineteenth century, however, when the cuneiform (wedge-shaped) scripts of Sumerian and Akkadian were decoded (a momentous event in the understanding of the history of the written word) both names could be uttered once again.

ABOVE: This ancient map of Mesopotamia, the land of Gilgamesh, dates from about 700-500 B.C.E. The tablet includes a description, in cuneiform writing, of the regions of the area and of the people and animals who lived in them.

THE HOUSE OF DUST

Many societies entertain an optimistic view about the afterlife, and share a belief that at least their heroes (or their saints) will thoroughly enjoy it. This is emphatically not true of the Sumerian civilization, nor of the Assyrian and Babylonian civilizations that succeeded it. On the contrary, once having set foot on "the path that allows no journey back" the human wayfarer is doomed to remain for ever after in the House of Dust (or Darkness), which "none who enters ever leaves" (just like Hamlet's "undiscover'd country from whose bourn no traveler returns"). This is a house where the inhabitants find that "soil is their sustenance and clay their food, where they are clad like birds in coats of feathers, and see no light, but dwell in darkness." This is how Enkidu dreamt of what was to befall him on the night before his death; and there is nothing in this passage or elsewhere to suggest that he may have been mistaken. No wonder then that it was not the afterworld itself but an unrealizable longing for immortality that was as close as Sumer got to an ideal of paradise.

THE ANCIENT EGYPTIANS FEARED DEATH AND WERE OBSESSED WITH THEIR EVENTUAL FATE. THEY WANTED TO LIVE FOREVER—AND BELIEVED THAT THEY COULD—BUT DEATH PRESENTED TWO DISTINCT ALTERNATIVES: UTTER DESTRUCTION, OR THE TRANSFORMATION OF THE LIVING, THROUGH DEATH, TO THE AFTERLIFE. THE EGYPTIANS HAD AN ETERNAL PLACE OF EASY LIVING THAT THEY CALLED "THE FIELD OF RUSHES." ALTHOUGH THEY REFERRED TO THIS PLACE AS "HEAVEN," IT HAS MANY OF THE FEATURES USUALLY ASSOCIATES WITH A PARADISE. BUT THIS WAS NOT THE ONLY AFTERLIFE ON OFFER: THERE WAS ALSO A HEAVEN IN THE SUN OR STARS, ANOTHER DESIRABLE DESTINATION UPON DEATH. A LESS INVITING OPTION WAS THE NETHERWORLD (OR UNDERWORLD), WHICH WAS OFTEN A HOSTILE ENVIRONMENT.

ANCIENT EGYPT

FRAGMENTS OF BELIEF

There are therefore three main destinies to consider: the heaven of the Field, the heaven of the stars, and the netherworld. Unfortunately, these three destinies do not fit neatly into a pattern of three alternative destinations. This is not so surprising, given that the religion of Ancient Egypt is often contradictory. In part, the confusion arises because the religion evolved over a 3000-year period, and new beliefs were added without old ones ever being completely discarded.

Modern scholars also have a different problem: because no single comprehensive record of belief survives (if indeed there ever was such a thing) a religious system has to be reconstructed from fragments of belief. These consist of hieroglyphic texts placed with the deceased in tombs and temples which were intended to help the dead in their journey, as well as spells written on papyrus or lucky charms which would protect the dead from evil. The Egyptians were, however, much more concerned with observing the rituals of death and assisting in the afterlife journey than in describing their ultimate destination, so unfortunately we have no detailed descriptions of paradise.

THE THREE DESTINIES

Egyptian faith revolved around the sun and the sun god Ra. To understand the three destinies of the afterlife, it helps to consider two important images: the daily journey of the sun, and the annual cycle of nature (which also relies on the sun). When the Egyptians watched the sun, they could see it in different places at different times: in the East when it rose, high in the sky at midday, and then out of sight in the

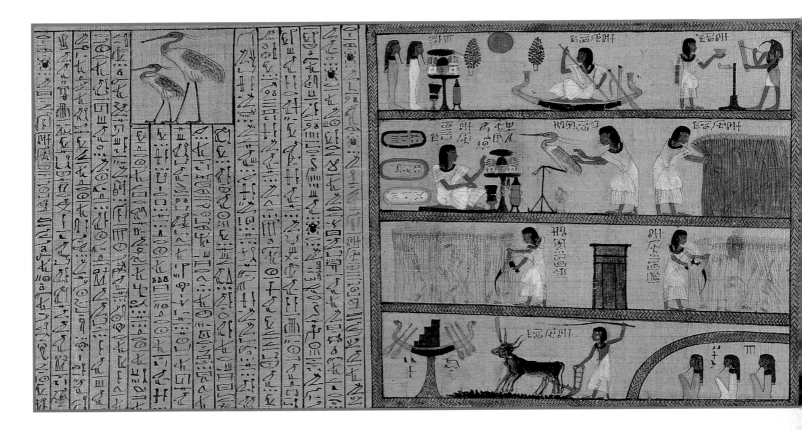

ABOVE: A papyrus from
The Book of the Dead
depicting the Field of Rushes.
This scene of eternal
harmony details the activities
of the blessed dead in a fertile
paradise, as they farm the
land and row on the
waterways and canals.

darkness of night. The different afterlife destinations related to the solar arc: the netherworld was linked to night; the Field to the sunrise; and heaven, of the sun and stars, to the daytime. In this belief system the netherworld, the Field, and the sun were all destinies for the soul. Just as the sun could be in different places at different times, so could the soul.

Ordinary Egyptians were not philosophers, so it would be a mistake to assume that their beliefs were logically reasoned through. It is likely that besides seeing these three afterlives as three different aspects of the sun's passage through the sky, they also, albeit contradictorily, saw the soul as residing permanently in one of these places: in the netherworld, where it is always dark; in the Field, where the sun rises; or along with the sun in the daytime sky.

By the time of the New Kingdom (c.1540–1075 B.C.E.), the Egyptians had added considerably to the idea of the soul's afterlife being a journey. Instead of being an ultimate destiny, the netherworld became a temporary destination on a voyage to a blissful afterlife. The deceased had now to pass through the netherworld and be judged. After this judgment (providing they gained the approval of the gods), the soul would emerge from the netherworld and never return to it. The common expectation was that they would emerge in the Field of Rushes, which was located on the Eastern horizon (where the sun rises). However, this did not prevent the Egyptians from also wanting to

journey to the sun. At the same time—again, contradictorily—the Egyptians continued to believe that the soul could be both in the Field and in the sun, depending on where the sun was in the sky.

Since the chief concern of this book is paradise, and because the idea of the judgment of the dead came late to Egyptian thinking, we will deal with the darkness of the netherworld after our exploration of the blissful afterlife. We turn first toward the fertile Field of Rushes.

THE FIELD OF RUSHES

"I know the field of rushes; its enclosure wall is made of metal... the east dwellers harvest there." The Book of the Dead

The Book of the Dead (also known as The Book of Going Forth by Day) is a collection of spells and guidance for the deceased that date mainly from the time of the New Kingdom (c.1540–1075 B.C.E.). It tells us much more about the precautions the Egyptians took to ensure an afterlife than about the nature of the afterlife itself, but there are short descriptions of the Field of Rushes (which is also referred to as the Field of Reeds and the Field of Offerings), from which we can piece together a picture of the Field.

We see from the quote above that the Field is associated with the East: the image is one of life and fertility; the Eastern horizon is thus the visual symbol of entry into this heavenly paradise—just as the sun rises, so shall the mortal be reborn. Other spells refer to the East as the "door" (or entrance) to the Field.

Surprisingly, although the Field is a place of life, it is not explicitly identified as a place of light, unlike the heavens of Greek and Hebrew traditions. It is, however, described as having a wall, which invites a comparison with the ancient Persian meaning of *pairidaeza*—a walled enclosure, and the origin of the word "paradise."

THE CITY AND THE RIVER

According to *The Book of the Dead*, the enclosure wall surrounding the Field is made of metal. This is probably an implicit reference to the Field's resemblance to

ABOVE: Solar barque being pulled across the sky toward the underworld, from the Tomb of Ramses III, c.1193-1162 B.C.E. Thebes, Egypt.

RIGHT: The surface of a gold sarcophagus. The Egyptians often decorated the sarcophagus with pictures of the significant events in the life of the deceased, and with mythical scenes explaining the separation between mortals and the gods.

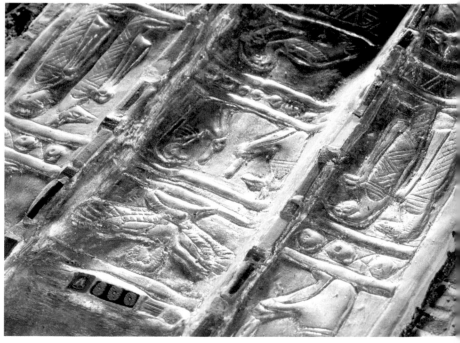

a city, which was a strong image of civilized and divine life for the Egyptians, particularly in the Old Kingdom (c.2900–2200 B.C.E.). In addition to walls, there are also roads: "beautiful roads which are in heaven, in the field of rushes." Elsewhere, instead of roads, *The Book of the Dead* presents an image of fields which are cut by waterways. Water also surrounds the Field. From *The Coffin Texts* (c.2170 B.C.E.), we learn that in making the journey, the deceased must cross a river. This "winding waterway" fulfills the same role as a wall: it is a protective boundary that must be crossed, an obstacle that must be overcome. The deceased travels to the Field in a boat, and the ferryman steering the boat asks questions which must be answered correctly before he will take the deceased to the Field.

THE BA AND THE BIRD

The Book of the Dead makes it clear that the waters of these passageways are pleasant, so that birds delight in being there. The presence of birds in this description is more important than one might initially think. The Egyptians believed that every deceased person had a *ba*. Essentially, the ba is the soul as it appears on earth after a person has died. This is not the same as the essence of a person when still alive—death is a transforming force—and thus the ba will not necessarily take a human form; in the Field of Rushes, the ba can appear in any form it likes. In Egyptian art, the soul was often depicted as traveling to the afterlife in the form of a bird; this must presumably have been a powerful image of freedom. Thus, in describing the waters as so pleasant that birds would want to congregate there, *The Book of the Dead* makes it clear that the Field of Rushes is a good final resting place for the ba—an afterlife to look forward to.

WORK AND PLAY

Another description in *The Book of the Dead* makes the reference to a divine city explicit, as the deceased yearns for a tranquil afterlife. Both a city and a field, the Field now also has a breeze and is a pleasant home:

"…Frequenting the Field of Reeds, of dwelling at peace in the great city, the mistress of breezes. May I be master there! May I be a spirit there! May I plough there! May I reap there! May I eat there! May I drink there…"

The Field is fertile, full of abundant barley with huge ears of grain, so we must assume that the water irrigates and helps to provide this crop. In addition to this crop, on arrival at the Field the deceased could—with the right spell—expect to be given certain items to make

ABOVE: *A detail from a painted wooden stela showing the soul of the deceased, the* ba, *as a human-headed bird. Late period, c.700-350* B.C.E.

his or her stay there easier; often this gift consisted of a loaf of bread. Some spells refer to the cake that will be eaten, others to the sexual intercourse that will be enjoyed, and still others speak of how the ba will be able to play games with those on earth.

Although the barley had to be ploughed, we should not think of this task as being hard work. Often, the Egyptians buried their dead with model "body doubles," and it was believed that these body doubles would act as servants to the deceased, performing all the necessary chores in the afterlife.

TROUBLE IN HEAVEN

Although accounts of the Field describe a prosperous afterlife in a fertile and easy environment (conjuring up an image of the cultivated Nile Valley), this heaven was not always so straightforward. *The Coffin Texts*, for example, talk of two goddesses who are the mistresses of Ra. They live in the Field and inspire love from the ba, which is dangerous for the ba because the goddesses collect power from souls and rob them of their magic.

It may also be a mistake to think of the afterlife in the Field of Rushes as eternal. Some tombs have been found with the inscription "I pass through heaven," suggesting that the Field may not be a permanent state. The phrase is also reminiscent of the passage of the sun in its eternal cycle of birth, death, and rebirth.

ABOVE: *Princess Nesitanebtashru ploughing with a yoke and oxen and reaping celestial grain in the Field of Reeds. Fresh running water surrounds the land. From the Greenfield Papyrus (the funerary papyrus of Princess Nesitanebtashru) and possibly drawn by the princess herself, c.970* B.C.E.

THE HEAVEN OF
THE SUN AND STARS

*ABOVE: The solar barque
of the sun god Ra crossing the
sky accompanied by his
attendants. Detail from a
painted wooden stela. Late
period, c.700-350 B.C.E.*

The earliest texts surviving from the pyramids date
from the Old Kingdom (c. 2900–2200 B.C.E.), and are
called *The Pyramid Texts* (c. 2500 B.C.E.). Written long
before *The Book of the Dead*, they stress the importance
of the sun, the essential Egyptian image of transformation and resurrection. The sun was depicted as a burning
red disk, or as being rowed across the sky like a boat.

The sun god Ra stands inside or on top. Ra may be in
human form, a man with a ram's head, or a scarab
beetle, pushing the disk of the sun between its forelegs.

At this stage in Egyptian history, ordinary mortals
could not aspire to heaven. The afterlife was restricted
to people of royal descent. The human Egyptian king
was seen as divine, and as Ra's deputy on earth. After
death, he merged with Ra in the sun-disk, or became a
star. There were various ways in which the king could
make this journey: in Egyptian art, the kings are
depicted as traveling on the wings of flying birds, rising
on smoke from incense, ascending on a raft made from
reeds, or climbing a divine ladder, the rungs of which
were made by the outstretched arms of the gods. Since
the kings did all they could to arrive at their immortal
destiny, we must assume that the journey was worth-
while. Over time, people began to believe that
ordinary mortals could share the same destiny as the
king, and ascend to the sun in the same ways.

The Tomb

*T*he Ancient Egyptians could not imagine that the soul could prosper in the afterlife without the body
continuing to exist; in other words, they had no concept of a separation between body and soul. The body
had to continue to exist. The tomb was the corpse's final resting place; it contained the preserved corpse and
often a model double of the corpse (if the corpse did decay, the double would ensure that the afterlife of the *ba*
and akh continued). The dead were often buried facing small openings in the tomb walls, which could serve as
channels of communication.

From the artifacts that were placed in the tomb (food, drink, pictures of gardens, various objects of daily use)
it seems likely that the Egyptians expected the afterlife to mirror life on earth, and that these possessions would
be carried into the next world. However, some scholars insist that these goods should instead be thought of
merely as offerings or provisions for the benefit of the body double.

*RIGHT: Clay figures from
a tomb. Kings and nobles
equipped their tombs with
treasures, possessions, and
models of their estates. Model
boats were often buried in the
tomb to enable the deceased
to join Ra by crossing the
sky, and to fish in the waters
of the Field of Rushes.*

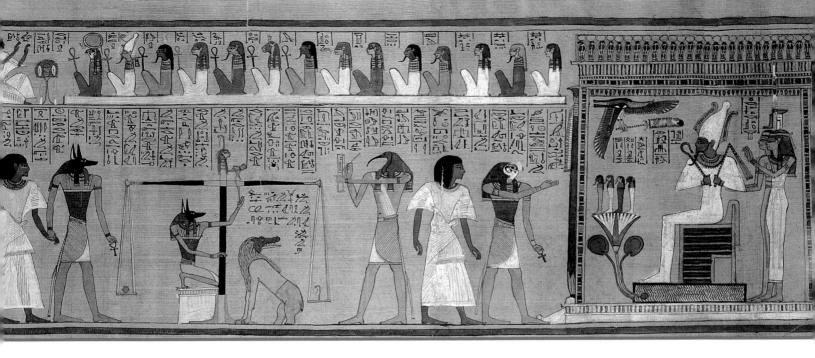

THE AKH

By joining the sun or stars, the soul became an *akh*. The akh (*akhu* in the plural) is the transfigured spirit that dwells in the sun or stars. To reach this heaven, the deceased (king or commoner) had to be armed with the correct spells. The spells imparted knowledge to the deceased and possession of them demonstrated to the gods that the deceased person had sufficient knowledge to become divine. The deceased were also equipped with hymns and prayers, which showed respect for the gods and helped them to be accepted as akhu, a transformation that was symbolized by the scarab beetle.

As glorified spirits, the akhu were withdrawn from the mortal world, in a distant but exalted existence. The akhu had some responsibilities: in its journey across the sky, the sun had to combat hostile forces. If, for example, it did not overcome the huge serpent Apophis, the sun would grind to a halt. The akhu assisted in this divine battle. Since the sun was often thought of as being moved along on a boat, the stars also assisted the sun's journey by pulling it along.

The akhu also gathered around the sun god, much as the angels of Christianity surround the throne of God. The akhu were not angels, however. The dead did not have to be "angelic" to turn into akhu, but they did need to believe in the gods.

We turn now to the netherworld, the lowest point in the sun's circle and the beginning of the soul's journey, to explore how the deceased was judged to be ready for the journey toward immortality.

OSIRIS: JUDGE OF THE DEAD

The netherworld, or underworld, was no paradise. Originally a place of monsters and other dangers (such as the perilous possibility of having to walk upside down), which had to be averted by spells, the nether-world evolved into a temporary destination in the journey toward immortality. The netherworld became associated with Osiris, an important god who increasingly became identified with the sun god Ra. Osiris was both ruler of the dead and the god of fertility, or nature. In Egyptian mythology, the god Osiris had been murdered and then resurrected (though the idea of an immortal god being killed seems strange today, to the ancient Egyptians the apparent contradiction seems not to have been important—if, indeed, it was seen as a contradiction at all). Having been resurrected himself, he became the cause of all resurrection. The ideas of ascension and the netherworld were now combined.

THE JUDGMENT OF SOULS

The dead stood before Osiris in the Hall of the two Truths. Osiris sat at one end, with all the great gods of Egypt sitting on thrones along the side of the Hall. There were 42 divine assessors or judges. To each of these judges, the dead (accompanied by the ba, who acted as witness) had to make a negative confession—for example, instead of saying "I have done good" the dead were required to say "I have done no evil." Sins included stealing, robbery, lying, anger, fouling running water (anti-social behavior in a society where this was the community's drinking water), sodomy, and cursing the king.

A great set of balancing scales was laid out in the Hall. The heart of the dead was placed on one side of the scales and a feather of truth (or law) put on the other. The ba stood close by, as did the goddess Ammut (who was part hippopotamus, part crocodile, and part lion), who devoured the dead who failed this test. As each negative confession was made, the scales were checked. The heart and feather had to balance. If they did not, the convicted was thrown to Ammut and died a second time. If the heart did counterbalance the feather, all was well and the dead could be rewarded: the ba could continue its journey toward an easy afterlife.

ABOVE: The Papyrus of Hunefer, *from* The Book of the Dead, *1294-1279* B.C.E. *shows the weighing of the heart and the dead's denial of sin in the judgment hall of Osiris, lord of eternity, who sits on his throne on the right of the picture. Ammut, the eater of the dead with the head of a crocodile and the body of a lion, sits to the right of the scales, waiting to eat the deceased if the scales do not balance.*

The Aztec empire, which evolved out of the Mesoamerican civilizations of the first millennium B.C.E., came into being in the mid-fourteenth century C.E., less than 200 years before its conquest by the Spanish conquistadors. The Aztec kingdom has many striking similarities to ancient Egyptian culture: the Aztecs built pyramids, believed in spells and magic, and wore protective amulets. Most importantly, the Aztecs also worshipped the sun. They frequently made human sacrifices to encourage it in its journey across the sky.

THE AZTECS

THE PARADISE OF TLALOCAN

The Aztecs believed in a paradise, Tlalocan, and in the heaven of Ichan Tonatiuh Ilhuijcan, but most mortals ended up with a less distinguished afterlife in the underworld, Mictlan, ruled over by the Lord of the Dead. Entrance to these places was contingent upon the cause and manner of death rather than upon behavior during life. For the Aztecs death, not life, dictated the nature of the hereafter.

Tlaloc was one of the first Aztec gods, dating from early Mesoamerican times, and one of the most important. As the rain god, he was closely linked to the cycle of nature and fertility, for crops could not grow without the rain that he brought. Tlaloc presided over the earthly paradise of Tlalocan so, unsurprisingly, the

Aztecs closely associated paradise with the water of the rain god, believing that all the lakes and rivers on the earth came from the springs which rose there. Tlalocan was a place of eternal abundance and permanent summer; the souls who prospered there enjoyed afterlives of leisure and pleasure, surrounded by nature. When they wanted to, they could return to earth as butterflies, to visit their loved ones.

Entrance into Tlalocan was exclusive, mainly restricted to those who had perished in the storms that Tlaloc sent, by being struck by lightning or through drowning. Those of the deceased who had gone to reside in the heavenly house of the sun were free to visit Tlalocan when the sun had set.

A different paradise, less important than Tlalocan but similar in nature, was reserved for innocent children who had died. Tonacatecuhtli Ichan was an idyllic garden paradise and, like Tlalocan, was full of flowers and trees.

THE HOUSE OF THE SUN

The Aztecs believed that the world and all living things contained an energy, a vital force, which they called *tonalli*, "the warmth of the sun." They also believed that the sun itself was engaged in a perpetual war against the powers of darkness and that the stars were opposing forces in this struggle. It was crucially important to assist the sun in its journey across the sky and ensure that it traveled across the sky without being stopped in its tracks.

The Aztecs routinely sacrificed their prisoners (sometimes as many as 20,000 in a single year) in order to release tonalli from the deceased which would then help to fuel the sun.

The Aztecs were a warrior kingdom and greatly valued their fighters, so it is not surprising that the task of the dead warrior was to help the sun in its eternal

BELOW: The Aztecs sacrificed their prisoners because they believed that energy released from the victims would help to fuel the sun and assist it in its journey across the sky.

struggle. For the first four years after their deaths, warriors lived in the heaven of Ichan Tonatiuh Ilhuijcan, the house of the sun, where they could assist the sun in its journey. At dawn, the dead warriors would meet on a great plain and greet the rising sun by beating on their shields. The warriors lived on the eastern side of heaven and formed a protective escort that ensured the sun's journey to its zenith. Having accomplished this, the dead warriors would then journey to Tlalocan, where they would spend their nights, before greeting the sun the following day.

After the four year period, the dead warriors descended to the earth and spent their time enjoying the fruits of nature as beautiful, brightly colored birds, and continued to welcome in the dawn with their song.

When the sun reached its highest point of its journey, the occupants of the West side of heaven took over as the sun's escort. Women who died in childbirth lived in the West for the first four years of their afterlife. They assisted the sun in its descent, bearing it on a litter of bright green feathers and ensuring the sun's happiness by issuing war cries. When the sun successfully reached the horizon, they fluttered down to the earth as moths. After four years, the dead women became hummingbirds and butterflies, and spent the rest of eternity on earth, where they could sip nectar.

BELOW: The Aztec lord of the dead, Mictlantecuhtli, represented in a 15th-century gold pendant—one of the few gold ornaments that escaped being turned into bullion by the Spanish conquistadors. The Aztecs understood the underworld to be a place without escape or redemption, dark and frightening.

The warriors and women helped the sun to rise and set and kept it moving across the sky. This was an effective use of tonalli. Most mortals, though, led undistinguished lives that could not assist the sun; consequently they never gained access to the house of the sun, but went to the underworld instead.

MICTLAN: THE REALM OF THE DEAD

Mictlan was the ultimate destination for Aztecs who died of natural causes or old age, presided over by the god Mictlantecuhtli and his female counterpart Mictlancihuatl. Although some scholars stress that it was a place of perpetual darkness, it is possible that the souls of the dead were thought to have access to the light, since the Aztecs may have believed that after the sun had set, it traveled through Mictlan to the East, where it could rise again.

To reach Mictlan, the undistinguished dead had to travel for four years on a hazardous route, crossing mountains and hills as well as encountering a huge snake and a giant lizard, before having to swim across a great river. This tiring process was probably important to the Aztecs because it showed that the dead of the underworld had wasted their tonalli in the efforts of their journey; they spent their eternity without the vital energy that was so necessary to the living.

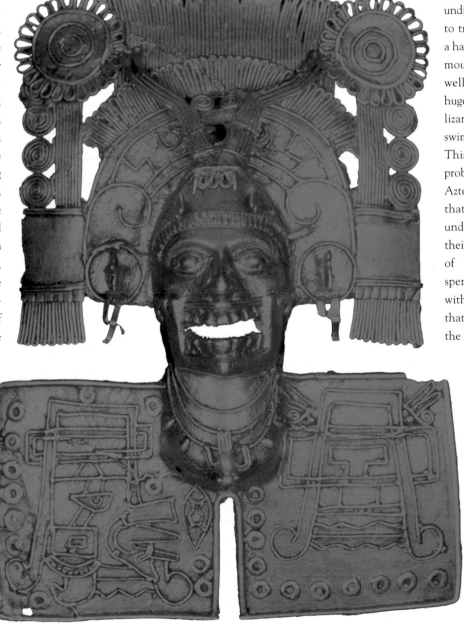

Traces of a Celtic civilization have been found as far back as the Bronze Age (late fourteenth century b.c.e.), but as a people the Celts first appear in central Europe, between the Danube and the Rhine, in the sixth century. At various times they migrated eastwards as far as Galatia in Asia Minor (modern Turkey) and westwards as far as Spain. But their most important migrations were west and north, to France (Gaul), Ireland, and the British Isles. The ancient Britons, of course, were Celts, and the French still distinguish their own Brittany (Bretagne), where some Breton is still spoken, from the large island across the Channel (Grande Bretagne). Irish and Welsh (and, to a lesser extent Scottish Gaelic) have stronger traditions to support them, for although the oldest sources relate to continental Europe the Celtic literary classics come from Ireland and Wales.

BELOW: Ancient beehive tombs on the Dingle Peninsula in County Kerry, Ireland.

THE CELTIC PARADISE

THE MIGRATION OF THE DEAD

The Ancient Celts envisaged the resting-place of the dead, especially fallen heroes, in two distinct ways. According to the first concept the dead remained in the graves in which they were buried, with their belongings by their side. In Ireland the grave was really a barrow or burial mound called a *síd*, which was thought of as occupied both by the dead and by their ancient gods, the Tuatha Dé Danann, dispatched to the underworld after their defeat by the forces of Christianity.

But the underworld was also a kind of Valhalla, in which fights continued to be fought by the dead heroes, buried along with their weapons. Some legends tell of heroes rising to fight again the day after their death.

The historian Procopius, born at the beginning of the sixth century C.E., tells a story which, he admits, "bears a close resemblance to mythology" (*De Bello Gothico*, IV, 20). "Along the coast of the ocean which lies opposite the island of Britta," he begins, "there are numerous villages inhabited by fishermen and farmers." This must be the west coast of Ireland. These villages assumed in turn the responsibility of escorting the souls of the dead to their final resting-place. The boatmen of the village whose turn it was remained in their houses after nightfall and waited to be summoned. Late at night there was a knock at the door and the voice of an unseen visitor was heard. Uncomplainingly they rose from their beds and without knowing quite how or why made their way to the shore where they found mysterious boats waiting, ready to cast off, but empty. On climbing aboard and grasping the tillers they suddenly became aware that the boats were heavily laden, lying so deep in fact that the water was a mere finger's breadth from the rowlocks. Yet they saw no one. They set off, and after an hour they landed upon the coast of Britta, a journey that in

their own boats would have taken them a day and a night. On reaching the shore the passengers disembarked, and the boats, now relieved of their cargo and riding high in the water, immediately set off for home. But whilst on the beach the boatmen had heard voices calling out the names of the dead souls, the positions of honor these had held, and the names of the dead souls' fathers. "And if women," Procopius concludes, "also happen to be among those who have been ferried over, they utter the names of the men to whom they were married in this life."

By "Britta" Procopius must have intended to refer to Britain (even though he habitually writes "Britannia") but this cannot be right. Setting off as they did from the west coast, the heavily laden boats with their mysterious cargoes must have been bound for some island or group of islands in the Atlantic, possibly the isle of Dursey on the south-west coast. The sources have a variety of euphemistic names for the realm of the dead: "the Land of the Young," "the Land of the Living," "the Land of Promise," and finally, most commonly, *Mag Mell*, "the Plain of Delights." The lord of *Mag Mell* was Tethra; the term "Tethra's Field," however, meant the sea: his domain included both.

AVALON

The Isle of Avalon is forever associated with the name of King Arthur, because Geoffrey of Monmouth, whose *British History* appeared somewhere between 1135 and 1140 C.E., says that this was where Arthur was carried to die after being wounded in his last battle. Geoffrey said a lot about Arthur; and his "history," based on Welsh traditions, was the starting-point of medieval Arthurian romance (the Welsh themselves said that Arthur did not die, but was waiting somewhere—perhaps Avalon—to recover enough from his wounds to be able to return to rescue his people). Geoffrey did not say where Avalon was, but when he introduced the

BELOW: Glastonbury Tor, Somerset, England. Glastonbury has long associations with Celtic legend, especially with the story of King Arthur.

THIS PAGE: These four pictures are from the first folio of a 15th-century French manuscript of The Romance of Tristan. *The first is of King Arthur himself. The others, clockwise, show the search for the Holy Grail, the Round Table, and the induction of a knight.*

name again in his *Life of Merlin*, he provided enough information to show that he, at any rate, did *not* think it was off the coast of Somerset, a claim that began to be made some time later by the monks of Glastonbury. This was recorded by a certain Giraldus Cambrensis, widely regarded as an astute critic and more reliable than Geoffrey. Writing of an attempt to find King Arthur's grave in the Abbey grounds, he explains that King Arthur died in Avalon, and adds that this was the old British name for Glastonbury. The name Glastonbury itself is Anglo-Saxon, but the name given to it by the ancient Britons (who were of course Celts) was *Ynys-witrin*, "Isle of Glass."

Nowadays it is possible to climb up the steep hillside to Glastonbury Tor from the town just below, and from there obtain an unrivalled view of the countryside for miles around. But in olden times, certainly at the time of Cymbeline, the first king of Britain, it was the hill itself that was called Glaestingaburg. And this hill was an island, the Isle of Glass, with the river Brue lapping at its foot.

The connection between Glastonbury Tor and Celtic mythology comes from a story in the *Life* of the Welsh Saint Collen, who lived in a cell on the slope of the hill. The summit of the hill was said to be

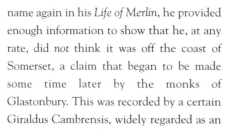

haunted by fairies, and one day Saint Collen boldly climbed up to confront Gwyn, King of the Fairies and Lord of Annwn, the realm of the dead. A fanciful legend of course, but one that indicates an ancient belief that Glastonbury Tor was where the dead were summoned to meet the Lord of Annwn.

So if Giraldus Cambrensis is right to say that Avalon was an old name for Glastonbury, it may have been an alternative and more cheerful way of referring to the rendezvous of the dead, the place where they passed over into a new form of existence.

Indeed the origin of the name Avalon may not be what Geoffrey of Monmouth says, the *Insula Pomorum*, the Isle of Apples, but the realm of Avalloc, another name for the Lord of the Dead. The identification of Glastonbury with Avalon rests, it is true, on a tissue of conjectures. But wherever it is to be placed, Avalon remains in Celtic mythology a blessed place that enjoyed perpetual summer, free from sorrow, and full of fruits and flowers, a place that needed no tending— an "Island of Delights," *Mag Mell.*

The Wooing of Étain

The beautiful Étain, who reappeared in at least two different incarnations, exemplifies metempsychosis, the transmigration of souls, one of the doctrines said to have been taught by the Druids, the learned priests of the Celts. First she was wooed by the elf king Midir, who emerged out of the lough (the Irish form of loch) on a dark brown horse, where Étain was bathing with her fifty noble companions. Midir was one of the gods of the underworld: his dwelling was a *síd* (burial mound) in Brí Léith in County Longford, which is where he invites Étain to follow him: "Will you come with me, white lady, into the wondrous land?"

In her second incarnation Étain was the wife of Eochaid, king of Ireland. Midir appeared to Eochaid and challenged him to a game of *fidchell* (a board-game similar to chess). They played three times, and Midir, losing on the first two occasions, uncomplainingly fulfilled the tasks he was set as a forfeit. The third game, though, he won, and demanded as his prize the right to put his arms round Étain to embrace her. Returning a month later to claim his prize, he found all the entrances barred. Undeterred, he made a magical entrance in the middle of the hall where the king and his warriors were feasting, put his weapons under one arm and then, picking Étain up in the other, disappeared through a hole in the roof. Looking out, the king saw two swans circling the house before heading in the direction of Midir's underground home.

THE VOYAGE OF BRAN

The Voyage of Bran is one of the earliest examples of the common Celtic genre of *immrama*, a term used to refer to stories of ocean voyages crammed with wonderful events and ending up in fairyland (the earliest manuscript of this tale dates from the eleventh century; the story itself must be older, and even in its oldest version may be partly Christian in inspiration). Bran, son of Febal, (who appears in the story with no further introduction) falls asleep one evening while listening to the sound of mysterious music. On waking he finds lying beside him a silver branch covered with white blossoms. The next day he receives a mysterious visitor, a woman who sings to him and his men of the glory and beauty of a land over the ocean to the west of Erin, an island supported by four golden pillars and full of all kinds of delights, including chariot-races held on a silver plain, the horses golden chestnut, roan, even sky-blue in color. There is no pain on this island, no sickness, no sorrow, no death. When the sea washes its waves against the land, crystal tresses fall upon the shore. This is where the mysterious woman herself lives and rules as queen over thousands of other women. The silver branch found by Bran jumps into her hand, and she disappears.

Bran then sails off with his companions, and after many adventures arrives at the Island of Joy (or Laughter). Leaving one of his men behind, he proceeds with the others to the Isle of Women that had been described to him. He and his companions receive a warm welcome. They go into a great hall where there is a bed and a wife waiting for each of them. They are treated to wonderful feasts in which all the food and drink has the taste that each one of them most desires; and they stay so long that they lose all sense of time. They believed themselves to be on the island for no more than a year, but actually it was much longer. One of Bran's men leaps ashore when they arrive home in Ireland and disintegrates into a heap of ashes, "as though he had been in the earth many hundreds of years." Bran is asked his name. "I am Bran, son of Febal," he said. "We know him not," comes the reply, "but the Voyage of Bran is one of our ancient tales."

This legend was later modified and its Christian elements expanded to form a new story called the Voyage of Saint Brendan. Brendan (known as the Navigator) was a real person, the founder and first abbot of Clonfert: he died in 576 C.E., and became one of the most popular of the long list of Irish saints.

BACKGROUND: Co. Donegal, Glencolmcille, Glen Head.

THE ORIGINAL VALHALLA, THE BLISSFUL HIGH-MOUNTAIN HOME OF GODS AND HEROES, WAS NOT GERMAN, AS DEVOTEES OF WAGNER'S RING CYCLE MIGHT BE INCLINED TO SUPPOSE. NOR DID THE IDEA ORIGINATE AMONG THE SCANDINAVIAN VIKINGS WHO TERRORIZED THE COAST OF BRITAIN IN THE EIGHTH AND NINTH CENTURIES. THE FIRST MENTION OF VALHALLA COMES IN THE EDDA SAGAS OF DISTANT ICELAND. FROM THAT STARTING POINT THE THREE TRADITIONS HAD GROWN AND INTERCONNECTED; THE SAGA OF THE NIEBULUNGS ON WHICH WAGNER BASED HIS FOUR-PART MASTERPIECE HAD ALREADY MODIFIED AND ADAPTED THE EARLIER LEGENDS, AND THE VIKINGS TOO HAD INTRODUCED NEW TWISTS INTO THE TALES.

VALHALLA

ABOVE: *Dead Vikings making their last voyage in the afterlife, to await Valhalla. Ninth-century bildstenar (carved stone) from the island of Gotland in Sweden.*

In the developed myth Hel is the goddess of the dead, sister of the wolf Fenrir and daughter of Loki. But Hel is first of all a place. Since "Hel" is an early form of "Hell" we might suppose that it must always have been thought of as a place of misery and gloom, the home of the wicked dead; but in the most ancient Icelandic traditions this was not so. One (admittedly contested) etymology connects "hel" with "hill," and "hill" with the barrows or grave-mounds in which the old Teutonic peoples buried their dead. If all humans, irrespective of the kind of life they led in the world above, were consigned after death to a nether world that was somehow identified with the grave-mound or tumulus that contained their corpses, then it is easy to comprehend the inclusive nature of this hell (or hill). To the seemingly paradoxical question that he raises, "Was Hel an abode of the Blest?" the scholar J.M. MacCulloch gives an affirmative answer: Yes, it was!

VALHALLA

The abode of the gods is Asgard, reached by crossing the rainbow bridge, Bifröst. Valhalla, the home of Odin, is the most splendid of its many palaces. Valhalla is undoubtedly a heaven of a sort, but since right of entry is reserved for those slain in battle this particular paradise has a more limited appeal than most. It is valor—not virtue—that gains you admittance, and since all warriors are males Valhalla caters exclusively for men. The only females to be found there are the Valkyries, who first transport the fallen warriors from where they are lying on the field of battle. Then, once the heroes have been welcomed by Odin, the lord of the gods, and installed in the great hall, the Valkyries stand ready to wait upon them.

The rafters of the great hall are made of spears, its ceiling is decked with shields, and its benches strewn with coats of mail. The warriors feast on the flesh of the boar Scrimnir that is placed in a great cauldron to be cooked afresh every day. Their staple drink is mead, served to them in goblets proffered by the attendant Valkyries. The mead never runs out, for it comes from the udders of the goat Heidrun, which chews incessantly at the branches of a sacred tree.

Valhalla is huge, with 540 doors from which 800 warriors sally forth every morning to do battle with one another, and then return after the day's jousting to the supper provided for them by the Valkyries. They will

Yggdrasil

In the whole of Norse mythology there is probably no more recognizably universal symbol than that of the great world-tree. The mighty ash-tree Yggdrasil supports the whole world. It springs from the body of the giant Ymir, who had been slain by Odin and his two brothers. It has three immense roots. The first of these reaches down into Asgard, the abode of the gods, the second into Jotunheim, where the giants dwell, and the third into Hel. Yggdrasil is sprinkled daily by the Norns with life-giving water springing from a fountain located beneath its ever-green branches. This is the fountain of Urd, whose waters are "so holy that everything which comes into this spring becomes as white as the skin which covers the egg and cleaves to its shell." Here too is where the wise Mimir drinks daily from another spring, a fountain of mead that is the source of wisdom and poetic inspiration.

live in this splendid palace until the Ragnarök (Doomsday), when they will march out of the doors for the last time to fight at the side of Odin against the giants. Whenever warriors in the real world fall in battle it is said that Odin needs them to strengthen his forces for the Ragnarök.

BELOW: Dead Vikings in the afterlife. Also from Gotland, Sweden.

The Death of Balder

Balder, the son of Odin and Frigga, is described in the early sagas as the best of the gods, "so fair and bright that a splendor radiates from him: he is the wisest, most sweet-spoken and most merciful of the gods."

Alarmed by a dream indicating that his life was in danger, Balder requested protection from the other gods, who gathered together and agreed to grant him invulnerability. This provoked the envy of the crafty Loki, who disguised himself as a woman and went to ask Balder's mother Frigga if it was true that all living things had sworn to do Balder no harm. Frigga replied that they had, with a single exception: the little mistletoe. Seizing his chance, Loki fashioned a dart from the mistletoe. Then he persuaded Balder's brother Hodur to join in the general sport of throwing things at Balder to prove his invulnerability. Hodur was blind, but Loki guided his arm, and the mistletoe dart pierced Balder and killed him. "It was the greatest misfortune that had ever befallen gods or men."

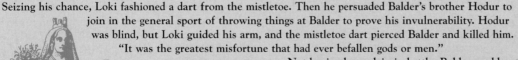

Not having been slain in battle, Balder could not go to Valhalla, but went instead to Hel. The goddess Hel agreed to release him, provided that "all things in the world' joined in bewailing him. They all did, except for one old witch, generally assumed to be Loki in disguise. So Balder could not after all escape from Hel, and will remain there until Doomsday.

CLASSICAL MYTH

THE ANCIENT GREEKS DID NOT LOOK FORWARD TO AN AFTERLIFE OF BLISS. INSTEAD, THEY EXPECTED TO ENDURE THE SHADOWY EXISTENCE OF THE UNDERWORLD, THE GLOOMY, SUNLESS REGION OF HADES. YET DESPITE THIS PESSIMISM, THE WORKS OF THE CLASSICAL POETS RESONATE WITH THE CONCEPT OF A PARADISE OUT OF REACH TO ORDINARY MORTALS.

Chapter 2

The poets helped to establish the idea of the lost Golden Age, the heaven of Mount Olympus and the sacred groves of the gods, the Heroes who win the respect of the gods and who, after death, reside in the idyllic Isles of the Blessed. Long after the decline of the Greek and Roman empires, these ideas re-emerged in the Renaissance as an inspiration to artists and poets alike.

LEFT: Mount Olympus, the highest mountain in Greece. The Ancient Greeks believed Olympus to be the heavenly home of the gods and that the mountain reached the sky.

GREEK PARADISE

THE IMMORTALITY OF THE POETS

The first and most influential Greek poets were Homer and Hesiod, who told their stories at festivals, feast days, and other important occasions and whose work was put into writing in the eighth century B.C.E. They never used the word "paradise"—because for them there was no such word. The word did not enter the Greek language until the fourth century B.C.E., long after these poets died, when the historian Xenophon returned from his Persian travels. He adapted the Persian word *pairidaeza* (a garden park, a walled enclosure) to *paradeisos*. The first use of the word describes the royal gardens of the Persian King Cyrus, with its wild animals and running water, and has no connotations of an afterlife; it was only after Greek translators had applied "paradeisos" to the Eden of the Book of Genesis that the word itself gained a spiritual dimension.

Nevertheless, even without the word, the poets did have definite ideas about places of eternal bliss and states of permanent contentment that can now be called paradises. These first appear in Homer's epics *The Iliad* and *The Odyssey*, as well as in Hesiod's much shorter *Theogony* and *Works and Days*.

Both poets expressed popular beliefs in their verse, but because the telling of good stories was far more important than being consistent within them, the two writers freely contradicted themselves as well as each other. In addition, they worked in an oral culture where stories were well known and could be freely adapted; themes about paradise might therefore evolve from one mention to the next. So a picture of paradise has to be built up from many sources—often from "throwaway" lines, combining the work of a number of poets and philosophers, including Pindar, Apollodorus, and Plato. The Roman writers Ovid and Virgil were strongly influenced by the Greeks, so this chapter concentrates mainly on their Greek sources but also shows how Roman writings developed the Greek concept of paradise, from a place that was out of reach to ordinary mortals to one that all people could enjoy.

BELOW: The Apotheosis of Homer, painted by Jean-Auguste-Dominique Ingres (1780-1876). Ingres depicts Homer as a hero and elevates the poet to divine status for being the father of modern literature. The women in red and green in the foreground represent The Iliad *and* The Odyssey. *The figures surrounding Homer include Plato, Alexander the Great, Shakespeare, and Mozart.*

THE GOLDEN AGE

The race of men that the immortals who dwell on Olympus made first of all was of gold. They were in the time of Kronos, when he was king in heaven; and they lived like gods, with carefree heart, remote from toil and misery. Wretched old age did not affect them either, but with hands and feet ever unchanged they enjoyed themselves in feasting, beyond all ills, and they died as if overcome by sleep. All good things were theirs, and the grain-giving soil bore its fruits of its own accord in unstinted plenty, while they at their leisure harvested their fields in contentment amid abundance.

HESIOD, *WORKS AND DAYS*

This passage is almost all that Hesiod had to say about the Golden Age, his first Age of Man in the Greek mythical and distant past. *Works and Days* is the oldest written source for the myth, which tells of a paradisaical but long gone period in human history. According to Hesiod, the Golden Men that the gods created lived long before Zeus (the supreme god) ruled on Mount Olympus.

Hesiod's description invites the reader to look back nostalgically to a lost age, when men lived like gods in heaven. They did not have to work—nature gave up its produce easily and in plenty—they never suffered or grew old. They did die, however, but gently and in their sleep. They died as they lived: mortal, but better than later mortals.

Hesiod makes it clear that following their deaths, the Golden Men were appointed by Zeus (who by now has usurped his father's authority) as divine spirits to guard over ordinary mortals.

Homer's view is slightly different from Hesiod's. In Homer's epics, the Golden Age is not completely lost: he tells of the Phaeacians and Ethiopians, content and peaceful peoples who share a warm relationship with the gods and enjoy their favors. Years ago the Phaeacians lived too close to the overbearing Cyclops (which dates them as being from before Hesiod's Bronze Age) so their godlike king Nausithous led the people away in a vast migration and settled them in Scheria:

Far from the men who toil on this earth he flung up walls around the city, built the houses, raised the gods' temples and shared the land for plowing. But his fate had long since forced him down to Death and now Alcinous ruled, and the gods made him wise.

HOMER, *THE ODYSSEY*

They live "too far apart, out in the surging sea, off at the world's end (where) no other mortals come to mingle." The virtuous Ethiopians live on the south side of the earth.

The happy race of Hyperboreans, according to Pindar, lived in everlasting bliss and permanent springtime in the northern area of the earth, beyond the mountains which were supposed to generate the north wind. They lived without disease or old age and did not fight or have to labor. This is strongly reminiscent of the lost Golden Age, with one important addition: they are out of reach by land and sea. The paradise of the Golden Age remains a tantalizing but inaccessible possibility, perhaps enough to boost the confidence of a nervous sailor—maybe I'll be shipwrecked, but look where I might be washed ashore!—but not offering an optimistic prospect of a future life. Greek myth and epic poetry looked nostalgically back, but it did not look forward. It was left to the Roman writers to inject a sense of hope, as they developed their concept of the afterlife.

A range of Roman writers, including Aratus, Tibellus, Virgil, and Ovid, all retold Hesiod's story and used him as their inspiration. Ovid added the theme of peace to Hesiod's vision of the Golden Age. For Ovid, there was no need for war; all people lived in harmony with one another and, free to do as they liked, led

ABOVE: Jupiter, the Roman equivalent of Zeus. As the most powerful of all the Greek gods, Zeus ruled and protected humankind from his home on Mount Olympus. Yet as a god of vengeance, he was respected more for his power than his morality.

naturally moral lives. The image is one of safety and protection from the outside; the Golden Age is a haven of tranquillity. In addition, there were no boats in Ovid's Golden Age, which meant that there could be no navigation across the seas. Without this travel, there was no possibility of anyone seeing a foreign world or a shore other than their own—so there would be no one to fight against. Instead, people could live free of cares, enjoying the fruits of nature:

The untilled field grew white with swelling ears of grain;
now there ran rivers of milk, now rivers of nectar
and yellow honey drooped from the green holm-oak.
OVID, METAMORPHOSES

THE SILVER AND BRONZE AGES

For Hesiod, the Silver Age followed the Golden Age, but was less paradisaical and therefore inferior to it. The Silver Men also lived on Mount Olympus, which implies a happy and privileged life. Yet this race did not enjoy the bliss of the previous age except in a long easy childhood that lasted 100 years, after which they reached adolescence. Then the trouble started: they died quickly, without reaching full maturity and they died painfully too—as they deserved to, because after their relaxed childhoods they lived immorally. The Silver Men habitually stole from one another and they showed a lack of respect to the gods, refusing to make any sacrifices or serve the immortals.

Nevertheless, Hesiod insists that the Silver Age was still blessed, and that despite the failings of its people, they should still be honored.

Next came the Bronze Age. This was a terrible stage in man's mythical past. Zeus fashioned the mortals out of ash trees and they worked bronze metal. They were violent and corrupt, strong but selfish, and they caused their own demise through their warmongering. Hesiod

says that eventually "dark death got them, and they left the bright sunlight." In other words, they went to the shadowy underworld of Hades, which was to the Ancient Greeks a miserable fate, an eternity of flitting through a place so miserable that even the gods avoided it. At best, it was a half-life: restless and ghostly, never-ending but also never enjoyable.

THE HEROIC AGE

The terrible nature of the Bronze Age helps to highlight the wonders of what came next: the Heroic Age, the inhabitants of which were noble, righteous, and godly. These qualities were to be expected, since the Heroes issued from relationships between mortals and the gods. They were therefore demi-gods, and were fortunate enough not to have to suffer the miseries of the underworld. On their deaths, they traveled to the Isles of the Blessed (also known as the Elysian Fields), a paradise of which we shall see more later.

The Heroes differ so strongly from the men of the Bronze Age that many scholars argue that this stage in man's past must have been inserted into Hesiod's story later. Certainly, it is helpful that this stage is here, because the mythical Heroes were the central characters in Homer's epic verse, so we can place them in the age that immediately preceded Hesiod's own, the Age of Iron.

ABOVE: In Homer's verse, the Sirens are two sisters who lure sailors to their deaths with their beautiful singing. On this early Greek vase, they are depicted as birds with women's heads. Tied to the mast, the Hero Odysseus is able to resist them. In later myths, the Sirens lose their femme fatale image and are depicted as beautiful women. In Plato's Republic, they supply the music of the heavenly spheres.

The River Styx

*B*elow is *Passage to the Infernal Regions* by Joachim Patinir c.1520. This famous Flemish painting combines classical mythology with Christian symbolism. Charon, the figure standing in the boat, is the ferryman of Greek mythology, who takes the souls of the dead across the River Styx to the underworld. Although Aristophanes describes the Styx as a swamp, and Dante calls it a black marsh, Joachim portrays the Styx as a blue, wide, calm river where the souls of the dead must make a moral choice. The human soul, the small figure sitting naked in the boat, must decide between two forks in the river: the one on the left winds a narrow difficult course that ultimately leads to heaven and eternal life; the one on the right is an easier path to hell. The angel on the left bank beckons the human soul to navigate the dangerous rocks and join it in heaven, but the boat is following the gaze of its passenger and gently heads toward the right bank. At first glance, this looks like an attractive place. Although the entrance is guarded by Cerberus, the monstrous watchdog of classical myth that here symbolizes the devil, it radiates the innocence of Eden. Yet hell lurks in the background, and the soul will soon be lost. Charon looks at neither heaven or hell but stares out of the painting toward the viewer, who will ultimately have to make the same decision.

THE PRESENT AGE

Hesiod laments his own wretched fortune at being part of this sad stage in man's history. Paradise, he sees, is sadly out of reach for him and his contemporaries. Instead, in this world, they have to endure incessant misery and harsh interventions from the many gods of Olympus. Man's fate appears terrible, predetermined, and inevitable. Adopting a prophetic tone, Hesiod reveals the signs which will show the ending of his age: babies will be born with gray hair, the gods of Decency and Moral Disapproval will abandon mankind in disgust and head home to Olympus.

Worst of all, mankind will no longer enjoy the possibilities of a content and eternal afterlife: death will lead to the underworld.

The Ages of Man myth shows that paradise is lost, part of the past; and even where the Golden Age still exists, it is out of reach. For Hesiod, it can therefore be nostalgically remembered; it cannot be regained. Hesiod's account does not say how long the Ages of Man lasted. More importantly, he never explains why the gods concerned themselves with mortals in the first place. To understand that, we need to visit Mount Olympus, the abode of the gods.

ABOVE: Roman marble statue of Apollo. As the son of Zeus, Apollo was patron of art, music, and poetry. According to Homer, he entertained the gods on Mount Olympus with his lyre.

OPPOSITE: Vulcan at His Forge by Peter Paul Rubens (1577-1640). Vulcan is the Roman equivalent of Hephaestus, the divine blacksmith and god of fire. His forge was believed to be on Mount Olympus, although Virgil places it in a cave near Sicily.

MOUNT OLYMPUS

…Olympus, where, they say, the gods' eternal mansion stands unmoved, never rocked by galewinds, never drenched by rains, nor do the drifting snows assail it, no, the clear air stretches away without a cloud, and a great radiance plays across that world where the blithe gods live all their days in bliss.
HOMER, *THE ODYSSEY*

As the highest mountain in Greece, Mount Olympus was an appropriate home for the hundreds of gods who lived there. The Ancient Greeks believed that Olympus was the highest mountain on earth and that its summit touched the sky. It was out of reach to mortals: an object dropped from heaven would take nine days and nights to tumble through the air, landing on the earth on the tenth day (this was the same distance as between the earth and underworld).

From the passage above, it is clear that Homer's Olympus is a place of relaxation and enjoyment where the sun always shines on the mountain summit, bathing the gods with light. Olympus is also eternal. But Homer's image of the gods living "all their days in bliss" should not be taken as the whole picture, for although the gods led an apparently idyllic existence, they spent much of their time in disputes with one another.

Homer and the other poets added many other details to Olympus. Mere mortals could never enter it; goddesses named the Seasons guarded the entrance of heaven, opening and closing the clouds to let the immortals travel in and out as they journeyed between Olympus and earth or came to attend one of the conclaves that Zeus held in the great hall of his palace.

Although the gods had their own homes, they also visited the house of Zeus on the summit of Olympus, regularly feasting there until sunset, eating the divine food ambrosia (which some scholars now claim was some kind of "magic" mushroom). The goddess Hebe, as cup-bearer to the gods, served them the divine nectar to drink, and Apollo, the god of music, played his lyre to the accompaniment of the Muses.

HEPHAESTUS

The god Hephaestus built the homes of the Olympian gods out of brass. As architect, smith, artist, and inventor, he also made the table and chairs that could move around Zeus' great hall of their own accord. He designed Zeus' thunderbolts—the symbol of the supreme god's ultimate power and authority—as well as jewelry for the goddesses.

To help the immortals travel to and from Olympus, he made the gold shoes that enabled them to travel at high speeds on both air and water. Often they traveled

by chariot; Hephaestus shod the horses' hooves with brass, which had the same effect as the gold shoes, and allowed the immortals to ride along the Milky Way— the divine road that led to Zeus' palace.

Mortals could not "fall" as the angels did from heaven, for it was impossible to reach the heaven of Olympus in the first place. Hephaestus, however, does drop from heaven to earth—though this was worse than falling: he was pushed. Homer tells the story early in *The Iliad*, where Hephaestus reminds his mother:

It's hard to fight the Olympian strength for strength. You remember the last time I rushed to your defense? He seized my foot, he hurled me off the tremendous threshold. And all day long I dropped…down I plunged on Lemnos, little breath left in me.
HOMER, *THE ILIAD*

Hephaestus' father is Zeus and his mother is Hera, Zeus' wife. His parents constantly quarrel. Hephaestus

foolishly involves himself in one of their arguments, which annoys Zeus; the father promptly throws the son to earth, causing him crippling injuries.

However, Hephaestus' story is not a true parallel of the fall from heaven: Hephaestus does not lose his stature as an immortal, and as he later re-finds favor with Zeus his fall is not permanent.

RIVALRIES IN OLYMPUS

The story of Hephaestus' exile tells us much about the Olympian paradise. Firstly, there is a great distance between gods and humans. This distance is not just geographical but also lies in the huge difference between immortal and mortal, between the infinite possibilities of Olympus and the mundane reality of existence on earth. Hephaestus is expelled to a place where he cannot trouble Zeus and Hera: earth. Secondly, Olympus is not necessarily very harmonious—there's not much of the "bliss" that Homer mentioned to be found in this story.

Paradises and heavens are normally expected to be places of ease and tranquillity, full of material and spiritual reward. Yet the way the Greek gods behave hardly suggests this. Zeus is more than capable of assuming all

his dignity as top god—with a nod of his head, he can shake Olympus to its foundations. He is capable of acting morally, he rewards and he punishes, he always holds great power. Yet—as shown by the reasons for Hephaestus' injuries—the gods argue with one another and there are all kinds of feuds and rivalries. There is plenty of time for the arguments: anyone residing in the Olympian heaven will never die. This is the fundamental unbridgeable gap between life on earth and life in heaven: the gods mold mortal destinies that they will never have to share. As for mortals, Zeus regards them with a certain detachment, as though human events are for his entertainment rather than his serious attention. Zeus watches over mortals, although eventually he lets them die. He sits on Olympus and sees them struggle through their lives.

Olympus is exclusively the heaven of the gods, but there are other divine enclosures linked to the gods. One such place is the Garden of the Hesperides, the sacred garden that belonged to Hera. It is far away from Olympus, but close to the subject of paradise. Like Eden, the garden contains a god, fruit which is dangerous to pick, and a serpent-like dragon.

ABOVE: On this Attic red-figure bowl (470 B.C.E.) Zeus and his eagle are seen carrying the beautiful youth Ganymede up to Olympus. As a symbol of Zeus's power, the sight of an eagle in the sky must have been a frightening portent to the Ancient Greeks.

ABOVE: *The Garden of the Hesperides from a 4th-century B.C.E. Greek vase. Ladon guards the tree. Because of the location of the divine garden in the far west of the world, the maidens who helped to guard the tree with golden apples were called "the nymphs of the setting sun."*

GARDEN OF THE HESPERIDES

"Atlas, a time will come when your tree will be despoiled of its gold by a son of Zeus…"
In fear of this, Atlas had shut his orchard up with solid walls and had given it to a huge dragon to guard, and kept all outsiders away from his borders.
OVID, METAMORPHOSES

The Islands of the Hesperides lie at the far edge of the ocean, therefore out of sight and out of reach to ordinary mortals. The Garden of the Hesperides belongs to Hera, but the immortal Atlas lives there. In this passage from Ovid, he is warned that a son of Zeus will steal fruit from the garden and therefore takes measures to protect it. The son of Zeus proves to be Heracles, who will soon be on his way to steal from the garden. Heracles should be regarded as a semi-divine Hero, which places this story in the time period of Hesiod's Heroic Age.

The garden's special quality is that it contains the tree which bears golden apples, a wedding present to Hera (these apples may be the reason why the fruit of the tree of knowledge in Eden, picked by Eve in the Book of Genesis, was later identified as an apple).

HERACLES IN THE GARDEN

Ovid combines motifs from different sources (especially Apollodorus and Euripides) to tell one version of the story: the tree and its golden apples are Hera's treasure, so the tree has been planted in her divine garden on Mount Atlas. She entrusts their care to the three nymphs (the Hesperides), who are permitted to live in the garden and protect them. These nymphs are beautiful maidens with wonderful singing voices. Their father is the Titan Atlas (the Titans fought with Kronos and against Zeus when Zeus dethroned his father to become supreme god; they are not therefore Zeus' favorite subjects); Atlas too lives in the garden, and is the orchard's gardener. When he hears that the apples will be stolen, he appoints the gigantic dragon Ladon to guard them, and protects the garden by turning it into a walled enclosure. This detail resonates with the original Persian meaning of "paradise."

Heracles is on the eleventh of his labors—a series of punishments devised so that he can atone for killing his wife and children in a fit of madness—and his present task is to pick the apples. He eventually reaches the garden.

Atlas is himself being punished for his part in the Titans' opposition to Zeus. He has to carry the sky—the celestial globe—on his head and shoulders. Heracles sets the sky on his own shoulders, on condition that Atlas picks the apples for him. Atlas is tired of his punishment and clearly will not want the sky back, but Heracles asks him to take the load for a moment, so Heracles can put a pad on his head and be more comfortable. Atlas obliges, but Heracles has tricked him and leaves the garden, with Hera's apples (the apples are eventually returned to the garden; it would be wrong to steal from Hera).

Here, then, is a garden that could certainly be described as a paradise. Punishment through work is a strong theme in the story: Heracles is performing a labor, Atlas has to toil under the weight of the sky (in the Book of Genesis this theme links closely to the idea of paradise). The garden also contains a dragon, though unlike the snake of Genesis it is not a tempter but a fearsome guardian.

AN INTERPRETATION

How are we to understand the story? To do so, we need to know what happens later. After Heracles' death, Zeus the father raises his son in a glorious ascension to Olympus, where Heracles resides as a god (although Homer places Heracles firmly in the underworld, rejecting the idea that even Heracles can have a happy afterlife). With Heracles' eventual destiny in our

Pandora's Jar: A Creation Story

"The woman unstopped the jar and let it all out, and brought grim cares upon mankind." HESIOD, WORKS AND DAYS

There is no paradise in the myth of Pandora, just blatant misogyny as Hesiod explains why there has to be suffering in his male-centered world: the gods create Pandora on Zeus' orders, as a trap for Prometheus, the Titan who made man from clay but then stole fire from Zeus as a gift to mankind. Pandora is beautiful, has great charm, wonderful clothes and jewelry. Unfortunately, the first woman has a "bitch's mind and a knavish nature." She is Zeus' punishment to all mortals who unwittingly accepted the gift of fire.

Prometheus' brother has a jar left over from the creation, which is full of unwanted horrors. Despite Prometheus' warnings, he falls for Pandora and lets her too close. One day (we must assume out of curiosity, without any idea that she is a punishment) Pandora opens the jar. Before she can close it, all the ills of the world have escaped apart from hope, which is all that remains as mortals battle against the hardships of life. Pandora is therefore "a great affliction" who ruins the world. Since Pandora is the mother of all women, Hesiod makes all women share Pandora's guilt.

ABOVE: *In the early 16th century, the theologian Erasmus turned Pandora's jar into a box in a basic confusion of language which merged the story of Pandora's jar with the related Roman myth of Psyche, who did have a box. As a result, the Greek myth is now commonly known as "Pandora's Box," a proverbial phrase that can refer to any act of unwise interference, and to a gift which is in reality a curse.*

*M*ost gods lived on Olympus but Pan had his home on earth, in Arcadia. Pan was physically ugly, with the horns and legs of a goat but this did not prevent him from seducing nymphs and drawing beautiful music from his panpipes, which he fashioned from reeds. He helped mortals to hunt, protected farmers' flocks but, essentially lazy, he also spent much of his time sleeping.

Arcadia was literally a district of Greece that was agriculturally poor, rocky and bare. As a result, the Greeks did not attach much significance to the area, believing that its inhabitants were unsophisticated and even stupid.

The Roman poets transformed Pan's home into the mythical Arcadia. For Ovid, Arcadia became home to the primeval savages that inhabited the earth before even the god Jupiter (the Roman Zeus) was born. They lived like beasts, were ignorant of art, and had no discipline or manners. Virgil, on the other hand, idealized the people and the area. They became representatives of a noble race that flourished in the lost golden age, living in a paradise of fertile groves and meadows, enjoying eternal spring and easy love as they communed with nature.

ABOVE RIGHT: An Arcadian god, Pan was the patron of shepherds and a fertility god, famous for his musical talent and amorous nature. Lord Leighton's 1862 picture of Pan playing his pipes originally illustrated Elizabeth Barrett Browning's poem "A Musical Instrument" in which, when Pan played his divine and seductive music: "The sun on the hill forgot to die / And the lilies revived, and the dragon-fly / Came back to dream on the river."

minds (and ignoring Homer's negativity), we can now interpret the dragon: by killing it, Heracles can steal the apples and fulfill his labors, which in turn will lead to his happy afterlife. The dragon is therefore the dividing line between mortality and immortality. By killing the dragon, Heracles effectively defeats death.

But what about the apples? The Renaissance artists were no doubt correct when they saw them as a symbol of vigilance: by keeping his wits about him, and managing to take the apples, Heracles shows that he is wary and on his guard, which are essential qualities of kingship. Episodes like this one help explain why Zeus can turn his semi-divine son into a full god.

THE FERTILE GARDEN OF CALYPSO

Homer's account of the Hero Odysseus' adventures in Calypso's garden offers a much fuller description of the joys and dangers of the sacred garden than does the story of the Hesperides. He frequently uses the image of a fertile garden to illustrate the similarities and differences between mortals and immortals: the fruits of the well-tended garden show the wealth of the gods—in the same way that a prosperous secular garden shows the wealth of its kingly owner—and suggest a civilized lifestyle. The divine garden is enclosed by natural borders which protect it from the possibly barbaric elements outside, and does not endure the natural cycle of birth, death, and toil. It is therefore both a place of bliss and unreality. Isolated and protected from the evils of the world, nurtured by the will of the gods, the garden

is both a haven from suffering and a sanctuary from the unpleasant. It is the rightful property of the gods.

A GARDEN OF SEDUCTION

For humans, though, the garden is also a place of temptation. As a rule of thumb: the more a mortal is seduced and tempted by the pleasures of the divine garden, the more he or she should beware of what is within. The tale of Calypso is a good example of this.

The nymph Calypso is another daughter of Atlas, and lives on the remote island Ogygia in the middle of the sea. The garden is impressive enough to hold even the gods spellbound—indeed, a god would gaze in wonder at nature's power and beauty. Spectacular woods mark the entrance to Calypso's cave. Alders, poplars, cypress, and cedar grow there; garden vines, grapes, violets, and wild parsley surround four springs of sparkling water. Owls, falcons, and sea crows roost in the grove. The secret garden provides Calypso with all she needs—not just wine and water, but all the ingredients of dishes that Calypso prepares for Odysseus to persuade him to remain on the island with her rather than return to his home in Ithaca.

Calypso is an enchantress, a temptress. She wants a mortal man, and wants Odysseus to desire her. She has saved Odysseus from the dangers of the sea and is reluctant to lose him. She may even feel he belongs to her. Using the fruits of her garden to bring him closer to her, she offers him immortality and eternal youth. Odysseus, although flattered by her attention, simply wants to return home. He knows that he is being held by force. With no boat, he has no escape and has the difficult task of resisting Calypso without offending her, as he does not want to incur her divine wrath. Eventually, he does leave with Calypso's blessing, in a boat made out of timber from her woods. He is saved by Calypso's fear that she might offend Zeus: while gods may sleep with women, Calypso knows that is dangerous for a nymph to sleep with a man; Zeus might get angry. Besides, there are other gods watching over Odysseus to protect him. One god speaks to Zeus; Zeus sends another god with a message that Odysseus should be freed. Calypso hears the message and reluctantly obeys.

Within the tale, it is clear that Calypso has a power verging on the divine, but Homer expresses her power through the strength and beguiling beauty of her garden. The garden is her own paradise. It is hers by divine right but not the place that Odysseus should aspire to. It was never intended to be a sanctuary for mortal man. This makes one wonder what happens after death to Heroes and ordinary mortals.

THE AFTERLIFE

THE ISLES OF THE BLESSED

Hesiod's Isles of the Blessed and Homer's Elysian Fields are one and the same, a resting place for the fortunate few who have the privilege of a blissful afterlife.

Homer's account of Elysium is similar to his description of Olympus—he regards it as the earthly parallel of life there. In this description there is no mention of the Golden Age yet clearly—as a place, and also as a way of life—the paradise of Elysium is also similar to the lost paradise of the Golden Age. For Homer, this paradise is reserved for the Heroes, who enter there without dying.

Just as the Golden Age is distant, part of the past, the Isles of the Blessed are also out of reach, located at the ends of the earth. This realm is far removed from the affairs of ordinary mortals, and once the Heroes arrive there and enjoy the blessed life they have no influence on the mortal world.

THE STORY EVOLVES

Long after Homer described his Elysian Fields, the idea of a blessed afterlife continued to appeal to writers who expanded the descriptions so that it became a land of flowers, sunshine, and happiness. The Greek writer Pindar, writing in the fifth century B.C.E., added the idea of the Fortunate Isles to the Isles of the Blessed, also introducing the notion of souls being judged in the underworld. It is a system of reincarnation: the bad are condemned but the good pass to the home of the pious, the Elysian Fields. For Pindar this is just a temporary stopover from where one can choose when to be reborn on earth. After living three good lives on earth, each time returning to the Elysian Fields, the soul is then free to travel to the Fortunate Isles (which is extremely similar to the Elysian Fields, just differently placed). Pindar's paradise is located on earth, but it is hardly "earthly": the final destination where the just and good can enjoy an easy life is reached through death.

ROMAN INTERPRETATIONS

The Roman poets picked up the Greek conception of the happy afterlife of the Elysian Fields and linked it with the Golden Age: in Virgil's *Aeneid*, the prophetic figure Anchises appears after death to tell his son Aeneas that he lives in Elysium amid the sweet assemblies of the blessed. Virgil (70–19 B.C.E.) dwells on the theme of the Golden Age: when Anchises forecasts the destiny of Rome, he predicts that Augustus Caesar, son of a god, shall again establish the Golden Age. Virgil does not specifically tie in his idea of the Golden Age with the Elysian Fields, but another writer, Horace (first century C.E.), does:

Jupiter (the Roman Zeus) set apart these shores for a righteous folk, ever since with bronze he dimmed the lustre of the golden age. With bronze and then with iron did he harden the ages, from which a happy escape is offered to the righteous, if my prophecy be heeded.
HORACE, *THE ODES AND THE EPODES*

Horace urges his audience to go "to the Fields, the Happy Fields, and the Islands of the Blessed," which implies that this afterlife is, finally, a place that all people can reach. The Christian religion would later adopt and adapt the idea of the Golden Age to embrace a belief in resurrection and heaven:

All crimes shall cease, and ancient fraud shall fail
Returning Justice lift aloft her scale,
Peace o'er the world her olive wand extend,
And white-robed Innocence from heaven descend.
POPE'S MESSIAH—CHRISTIAN HYMN

...the deathless ones will sweep you off to the world's end, the Elysian Fields... where life glides on in immortal ease for mortal man; no snow, no winter onslaught, never a downpour there but night and day the Ocean River sends up breezes, singing winds of the West refreshing all mankind.
HOMER, THE ODYSSEY

BELOW: *Mercury in the Elysian Fields, a third century C.E. fresco from the hypocaust of Octavius. As the divine messenger of the gods (Hermes to the Greeks), Mercury was also guide to the dead and escorted the souls of the dead to the afterlife.*

*G*iven the miserable nature of the Underworld, it is hardly surprising that many Greeks wished to find something better to look forward to in the afterlife. They turned to the Mysteries and the promise of paradise.

The first Mystery tradition, the Eleusinian cult, dates from around 1800 B.C.E.; under the guidance of a High Priest, its followers revered the corn goddess, Demeter. At first the cult members observed secret rites and ceremonies simply to ensure an abundant harvest and their own prosperity.

However, by the seventh century B.C.E. and the Homeric Hymn to Demeter (attributed to Homer but not written by him) the focus of the Eleusinian cult had shifted from nature's renewal to the renewal of the soul in the afterlife: initiates received esoteric truths, watched mystery plays and ritually participated in knowledge that would in due course lead them to the paradise of the Elysian Fields. During the initiation ceremony, new followers symbolically died and journeyed through the underworld to emerge, reborn, with a guaranteed afterlife of prosperity and ease. Whereas Homer's epics had insisted that only the Heroes would enjoy the Elysian Fields, the Mysteries made this paradise available to ordinary mortals, provided they were initiated into the cult.

The Eleusinian Mysteries stressed the importance of secret truths (the exact nature of which did not survive the movement and are therefore unknown to us). The quote below, from the ending of the Homeric Hymn to Demeter, shows that the fruits of agriculture were closely linked to the Mysteries. The Greeks believed Demeter to be responsible for agriculture and many scholars believe that the Mysteries were linked to the agricultural cycle and the bounties of nature. While the Hymn emphasizes that Demeter revealed the Mysteries, it maintains the secrecy of the movement and does not reveal them to the listener (the inappropriate telling of the Mysteries was a sin punishable by death). The Hymn laments the future fate of the uninitiated who have not participated in the rituals of the Mysteries and who will therefore after death have to endure the dreary darkness of the underworld. The initiate escape this fate: by participating in the rituals they are blessed.

Originating in the seventh or sixth century B.C.E., the Orphic cult added an ethical dimension to the idea of paradise. The cult was based on poems (now lost) attributed to Orpheus, a mythical figure who journeyed to the underworld after the death of his wife to rescue her. He was unsuccessful because he failed to observe the condition of her release, that he should not look at her until she had rejoined the realm of the living.

The Orphic rituals stressed the importance of moral purification. Participants had to rid themselves of evil, because the bad (or impure) would suffer the afterlife of the underworld, whereas the good (the pure) would enjoy the paradise of the Elysian Fields.

While many cults emphasized the importance of good conduct, the cult of Dionysus (the Greek god of wine) went to the opposite extreme. The initiation rites reflected the mythical life of a god who enjoyed drunken orgies and provoking mortals to frenzied sexual ecstasy, a very different kind of paradise. During the ritual ceremonies, mystery plays were performed which would lead participants to a blissful afterlife. When the Romans incorporated the Mysteries into their own belief system, they also welcomed Dionysus with open arms. Bacchus, the Roman equivalent to Dionysus, gained in popularity during the first century B.C.E. but is most strongly associated with a later period: the decadent decline of the Roman Empire and the excesses of the Emperor Caligula.

OPPOSITE: Demeter with Persephone presenting corn to the mortal Triptolemos, from a relief on a tomb at Eleusis, c.440-430 B.C.E. The Greeks often represented the corn goddess Demeter with ears of corn and a scepter. The Eleusinian mysteries may have been based on the myth of Demeter's search for her missing daughter, Persephone. In the myth, Demeter grieves for her daughter at Eleusis.

"Demeter made fruits spring up from the rich plowlands, and the whole world became heavy with leaves and flowers. Then she went forth to the kings... to them she showed the perform- ance of her rights and taught her Mysteries—holy rites that are awesome, that no one may transgress nor reveal nor express in words... Whoever among men who walk the earth have seen these Mysteries is blessed."

HOMERIC HYMN TO DEMETER

TEMPORARY STOPOVERS

Chapter

3

The Pure Land tradition of Buddhism pictures a blissful region of perfect happiness in an idyllic environment free from danger, suffering, and all kinds of evil. Hinduism, which postulates a variety of heavens, each associated with a particular god, also speaks of a long-vanished paradisaical age that will one day return again.

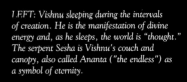

LEFT: *Vishnu sleeping during the intervals of creation. He is the manifestation of divine energy and, as he sleeps, the world is "thought." The serpent Sesha is Vishnu's couch and canopy, also called Ananta ("the endless") as a symbol of eternity.*

Buddhism was founded by Siddhatta Gotama (c.563–483 b.c.e.), who lived and taught in North India and was given the title "The Buddha" (The Enlightened One) by his followers. The Buddha's teachings are complicated and highly philosophical and form the basis of both Theravada and Mahayana Buddhism, the two main branches of Buddhist belief that themselves contain numerous sects.

BUDDHIST PARADISE

Theravada Buddhism, generally speaking, follows the original teachings of the Buddha more closely than does Mahayana, and the Buddha's teachings have little to do with paradise. For the Buddha, there was no lost golden age to yearn for and no ultimate destiny in a fertile garden to strive toward. While he believed in the existence of gods, he did not consider them worthy of worship since the gods are not in control of human destiny. For the Buddha, there was no supreme deity who would generously bestow gifts of immortality or even divinity on humans.

There is, moreover, no possibility of attaining paradise on this earth or in one's lifetime. For the Buddha, existence consists of suffering, and the realities of human life—such as disease, old age, and death—are unsatisfactory. He taught that it is possible to free oneself from the endless cycle of birth, death, and subsequent reincarnation that appears to determine all existence. To achieve this, one must shed the shackles of greed, hatred, and delusion that spring from desire and attachment. The achievement of this liberation is nirvana, which means "extinction" or "blowing out" although it is often described as "bliss." Nirvana is not death, nor is it paradise. Many modern Buddhists understand it to be the destruction of all sense of self.

If Buddhism were nothing but this, discussion of it would end here, with the acknowledgment that the Buddha's uncompromising teachings—primarily addressed to ascetics and monks—did not allow for desires of any kind, not even the desire for a paradise, heaven, or blissful eternity. Yet within Mahayana Buddhism a much more comforting view gradually emerged which, for the laity at least, moved away from the rigorous emphasis on the importance of achieving nirvana and began to portray the idea of a succession of attractive rebirths in ever more heavenly realms. The ultimate goal remained the same, to achieve nirvana. People unable to do this in this world would stand a better chance if they were reborn in a better next world.

Paradise came to Buddhism not as a permanent destiny of immortal bliss but as a blissful temporary stopover in the journey toward enlightenment: a Pure Land.

BELOW LEFT: The Buddha Amitayus, 18th-century Tibetan bronze. Usually identified with the Buddha Amithaba, Amitayus is the Buddha of Eternal Life, the Buddha of the Western Land. His name is invoked for health, happiness, and long life.

BELOW: A 17th-century Japanese depiction of the death of the Buddha. At his death, the Buddha entered parinirvana, the final extinction. According to tradition, his body ignited itself after his death.

THE BUDDHA AMITABHA

The first Pure Land teachings were written in India in the second century C.E., spread to China and re-emerged in thirteenth-century Japan. They require faith in the Buddha Amitabha, the Buddha of Measureless Light. This is not the same Buddha as the founder of Buddhism—a Buddha is someone who has achieved nirvana but whereas the historical Buddha operated in this world, the Buddha Amitabha operates in a distant and completely separate universe far in the west. Amitabha grants sentient beings rebirth in his sphere of influence or "buddha field," a miraculous paradise known as the Pure Land.

According to the *Sukhavativyuha Sutras* (teachings), before he became the Buddha Amitabha and having already been reborn countless times, Amitabha had in one life been a monk named Dharmakara. Dharmakara vowed to become a Buddha. In doing so he became a Bodhisattva (the Bodhisattvas are a little like the Christian saints, figures who have dedicated themselves to achieving buddhahood and to ensuring the salvation of others). Dharmakara made 48 vows about what his buddha field would be like. After many subsequent rebirths he achieved enlightenment and he created his own buddha field, a wonderful paradise that contains the best elements of all the buddha fields he had visited in his rebirths and is therefore far superior to anything found on earth. There are no miseries in Amitabha's abode of bliss: indeed it is so wonderful that one could look forward to being in it not as a means to the end (nirvana) but as an end in itself.

DHARMAKARA'S VOWS

The *Longer Sukhavativyuha Sutra*, one of the main Pure Land scriptures, describes in some detail the promises that Dharmakara made about his buddha field. These vows give a clear idea of the philosophy of Pure Land believers. One vow states that all living beings who dedicate themselves to being reborn in his buddha field will indeed be reborn there, even if they have made this resolution as few as ten times. In medieval Japan, where Amitabha was known as Amida, Pure Land

monks simplified this still further. Whilst the vow suggests that to be saved into Amitabha's paradise it is necessary both to live well and to believe (a doctrine that combines the importance of good works with the need for faith), other monks taught that repeating the mantra *Namu Amida Butsu* ("homage to Amida the Buddha") was in itself enough to ensure that the Pure Land follower would enter this paradise. Indeed, anyone who recites this phrase will be guaranteed entry into the Buddha Amitabha's paradise.

> *There shall be no distinction, no regard to male or female, good or bad, exalted or lowly; none shall fail to be in his Land of Purity after having called, with complete faith, on Amida.* HONEN SHONIN

Another vow states that the Buddha Amitabha will appear at the moment of death to all those that aspire to enter paradise, trust in the Buddha, and are committed to becoming enlightened. The Buddha will stand before them, accompanied by a retinue of monks, so that they can meet their deaths without anxiety.

As a result of this vow, Pure Land believers can have confidence in their next rebirth, dying peacefully and looking forward to paradise. Part of Pure Land belief is that it is possible to predict one's own death in advance and to prepare for it. Amitabha often appears in visions or dreams to reassure and prepare the dying person for his or her death. The dying person may experience some of the features of the Pure Land: unusual and delightful scents, colored lights, celestial music, or flowers may surround the dying person when, as the vow promises, Amitabha comes from his western paradise. In addition, relatives of the deceased receive reassurance that their loved one has indeed entered Amitabha's buddha field. Not only might the dying person announce that the Buddha is coming, but the relatives might dream of the rebirth in the Pure Land, when the deceased emerges from a lotus flower. Alternatively, the deceased may return to the relatives in dreams, telling them that he or she has been reborn into the Land of Bliss.

RIGHT: A banner from 981 C.E. depicting Kuan-Yin of the Thousand Arms. In Chinese Buddhism, Kuan-Yin is the Bodhisattva of compassion, the "spiritual son" of the Buddha Amitabha, and he came to embody feminine virtues. He dwells on a mountain from which he can hear the suffering cries of sentient beings. On his tiara is an image of the Buddha Amitabha. He has eyes in the palms of his hands which allow him to see everything within creation and is here surrounded by images of benevolence.

MEDITATION AND VISUALIZATION

It is not necessary to die in order to have a vision of the Buddha Amitabha or the Pure Land. Alongside the *Sukhavativyuha Sutras* is another important teaching, the *Visualization Sutra*. This key text provides a way for believers to access the Pure Land paradise in their own lifetime, to have a vision of the buddha field, and to behold the Buddha Amitabha accompanied by his attendants. The *Vizualization Sutra* is a manual of meditation which enables the user to visualize paradise in this lifetime and to be mindful of the Buddha. By using it, believers will ensure their own rebirth in the land of bliss.

The sutra is designed to help the believer to develop an exact and complete mental picture of the land of bliss; it therefore goes into considerable detail about the characteristics of the Buddha and his field. In the meditation, the Buddhist envisions stage by stage the key components of the Land of Bliss, such as the setting sun, water, the ground, bodies of water, and trees. It also enables the meditator to envision the Buddha and his Bodhisattva attendants.

The Buddha Amitabha is as bright as the sands of heaven and huge in stature. Between his eyebrows is a large tuft of white hair. His eyes are like pure clear oceans. Around his head is a circle of light. The sutra stresses that the Buddha has 84,000 physical characteristics, each of which sends out a ray of light. The light spills out in all directions and embraces all those who are mindful of the Buddha.

The details of the Land of Bliss vary slightly from sutra to sutra; we turn now to the nature of the Buddha Amitabha's paradise as described in the Sukhavativyuha Sutras.

THE PARADISE OF THE BUDDHA AMITABHA

The Pure Land lies in the distant west, 100,000 million buddha fields away. Within it, there is a total absence of evil and suffering. Its inhabitants know only happiness. Even the environment presents no hazards: there are no storms, no treacherous mountain passes, or dangers of any kind.

Decorated with gold, silver, emerald, and crystals, the Field is enclosed by rows of railings and palm trees or, in the longer sutra, by banana trees, palm trees, and a screen of golden netting (the descriptions of paradise as an enclosure have left scholars debating the extent

ABOVE: A Tibetan mandala, which is used as a device to aid meditation.

LEFT: A 17th- or 18th-century Japanese statue of the Compassionate Bodhisattva Ksitigarbha. In a tradition which has parallels to Pure Land but is not connected to it, Ksitigarbha's name is invoked to save sentient beings from hell.

to which the Pure Land school were influenced by the Persian concept of the *pairidaeza*). The trees are adorned with tinkling bells. These decorations are the roots of merit of the inhabitants of the Field.

Trees also surround the ponds of the Field. The ponds are built from the same precious materials that decorate the Field itself, as well as pearl, sapphire, and mother of pearl. Golden sand covers the bottom of the ponds and the huge blossoms of lotus flowers add intense colors to the gentle waters that fill the ponds. The waters are cool and refreshing, ideal for bathing, and a swim is made easier still by the elegant and expensive stairways that rise up at the edge of the pools.

In addition to the tinkle of bells on the trees, there is the constant sound of music. Wild birds add to this music, tunefully singing the praises of the Buddha three times each day, then three times each night. This background chorus encourages the inhabitants to think of the Buddha Amitabha's splendor. The Field also contains hundreds of thousands of vases, made from different kinds of gems and containing many kinds of wonderful fragrances, which reach far into the atmosphere and assist worship.

There are clouds in the Field and there is rain too—but not of the ordinary kind. The clouds play music (or perhaps are music) which enchants the Field with its beauty. The rain falls as sweetly scented flowers that are like beautiful jewels, and all the gems of the buddha field exceed in value anything found in our world.

As well as the jewel trees that adorn this paradise— the longer sutra goes into great detail describing the wonders of the trunks, branches, and leaves, and how they are made from different combinations of wonderful jewels and precious metals—the field is covered in flowers, which are soft and deep, like a carpet that rises to your ankles as you walk on it.

There are also huge lotus flowers. The lotus is a favorite plant of Buddhism because it opens to receive the sun. In Amitabha's field, they are made from precious gems. Unsurprisingly, given that the Buddha of the Land of Bliss is the Buddha of Measureless Light, millions of rays of light burst out from the plants in every direction. At the end of each ray is a golden Buddha, and each of these Buddhas visits a new world in order to enlighten its inhabitants.

Rivers are an important feature of this paradise. Varying in width and depth, they all flow gently and bejeweled flowers float on them. The waters are scented and make moving sounds of soft pure music which can be heard by all the occupants of paradise.

The Tree of Awakening

A massive Tree of Awakening stands at the center of the field, four million leagues high, with branches that stretch out for two million leagues. Splendid in its beauty, the Tree of Awakening is visible to all the occupants of the Land of Bliss. The tree is covered with jewels and brightly covered garlands and is covered by a golden net.

A gentle breeze stirs the tree, creating the sounds of the true principles of Buddhism. Anyone who has encountered the tree through all the senses (hearing it, seeing it, smelling it, being touched by its light, and meeting it through mind and thoughts) will remain pure and untouched by suffering or disease until they achieve nirvana. They will never stumble in their journey toward nirvana, especially if they use the Tree of Awakening in their meditations.

This tree is therefore an essential part of paradise. It is more spectacular but conceptually similar to the Bodhi (or Enlightenment) Tree of the historical Buddha in India, under which he resisted the temptations of the king of the demons, Mâra, and himself became enlightened. The Bodhi tree was a sacred fig tree, *ficus religiosa*.

Yet if anyone decides not to hear the music, then the sounds of the river will not reach that living being. If someone stands on the river bank and wishes to hear words instead of music, he or she will do so and can choose which words will be audible. All the words they hear fall within the realm of the spiritual and contribute to paradise: in the Land of Bliss, one will never hear the word "suffering," for there is none, but will enjoy words like "joy," "serene," and "unborn" instead.

Just as the occupant of paradise decides on the music and words, so when a bather steps into the waters of these rivers the water adapts to the wishes of the bather. It becomes as deep or shallow as is desired, as warm or cool as the bather wishes. The rivers are therefore a place for spiritual entertainment and blissful delight, free of any impurity and attracting all kinds of singing birds.

Bathing is just one of the joys on offer in the Land of Bliss. The inhabitants of paradise will have whatever they wish for, be it a garden to walk through, a palace to live in or a pavilion to visit. If they want perfume or parasols or musical instruments, fine clothes or jewelry, these things will appear for them. They may choose the dimensions, design, and content of their palaces, and all the canopies and cushions. They live and play in their palaces, surrounded by thousands of nymphs.

The living beings in the Land of Bliss are more like gods than humans. They are of great stature, are filled with merit and have powers and strengths that far exceed those of earthbound mortals. They do not have to eat to be nourished—whatever food they desire, they visualize, and as soon as they do so, the food is already consumed by their bodies.

OPPOSITE: Nineteenth-century Indian painting depicting Vishnu as the whole world, the being from whom all things emanate.

HINDUISM AND BUDDHISM BOTH HOLD THAT THE GOOD AND EVIL ACTIONS OF ONE'S LIFE DETERMINE THE NATURE OF ONE'S SUBSEQUENT REBIRTH. MOST PEOPLE REMAIN IGNORANT ABOUT THE TRUE NATURE OF THE UNIVERSE: THEY CHOOSE LIVES OF WORLDLY PURSUITS AND REMAIN TRAPPED WITHIN THE CYCLE OF BIRTH, DEATH, AND REBIRTH. HOWEVER, IT IS POSSIBLE TO ESCAPE FROM THIS PATTERN.

HINDUISM

ABOVE: In this 18th-century Indian illustration, the god Krishna dances in a glade to music played by three girls, and peacocks nest in the trees. Krishna is depicted as a good-looking and well-dressed youth. He lived among herdswomen and dallied with them; in later myth he is said to have become attracted to his own good looks.

Unlike Buddhism, which rejects the idea of the soul, in Hinduism every living being has an eternal spark of the Ultimate. The soul spark is *atman*; the Ultimate or Absolute is *Brahman*. By good action one can reach the Ultimate and thus become free from the cycle of rebirth. This is the goal of life and is salvation, but it is not paradise, although it is eternal and blissful in nature.

That said, the idea of paradise is much more prominent in Hinduism than in Buddhism. Within Hinduism, a distinction must be made between the paradise of the world ages and the heavenly paradise reserved for those who enjoy a temporary stay in the heavens before being reborn on earth.

THE WORLD AGES

There are four world ages, called *yugas*, similar to the four ages of the Greek tradition (see the Golden Age on page 33). Named after the throws of an Indian dice game, they are called *krita*, *treta*, *dvapara*, and *kali*. Each of these yugas is shorter than the one before, matching the decline in behavior and standards.

The Hindu paradisaic age is krita, the winning throw, the number four. It lasts 4000 divine years (each divine year is 360 human years) with a dawn and twilight period of 400 divine years, which is the transition period between one age and another and in which the character of both ages can be found. In the age of krita, virtue reigns. Intellectually and physically, people live as giants and a lifespan lasts 4000 mortal years. There are no quarrels or wars, for everyone is happy in this age of truth and righteousness as they observe the fundamental moral laws of the universe, the Dharma.

Hindus believe that we are now living in the kali-yuga, the darkest age of the cycle, righteousness having declined in the ages of treta and dvapara to this period of vice, depravity, and neglect, typified by short

lifespans, discord and disease. The age began in the fourth century B.C.E. Including the periods of dawn and twilight, there are nearly 427,000 mortal years before the end of the present age, at which point the earth will be destroyed by flood and fire. The earth will then be re-created, with the dawn of a new paradisaic krita-yuga. The cycle repeats endlessly.

THE DIVINE ENCLOSURE

The Hindu heavens are situated in the divine enclosure Ilavrita, which is said to be located to the north of the Himalayan mountain range. At the center of the enclosure, which is also the center of the entire Hindu universe, is the mythical golden mountain, Mount Meru.

Standing 160,000 leagues tall, Mount Meru is the highest point on earth and is believed to be the source of the celestial river Ganges, which divides into four terrestrial streams that flow to the four points of the compass. Close to Mount Meru rises the mountain Suparsva, and its celestial grove in which the deities amuse themselves.

Brahma-loka is an important part of heaven, and contains the remote "abode of truth" where the god Brahma meditates. Only Brahma fully comprehends Mount Meru. Brahma-loka also houses figures that are not unlike the Christian saints, *prajapatis* who will never return to the earth because they have escaped reincarnation and are beyond rebirth.

THE BRIGHT REALM

The Bright Realm, Svar-loka, is the region of the abodes of the gods, situated on or around Mount Meru. The deities reward their mortal followers by inviting them to live in the bright realm until they are reincarnated. The paradises are places of pleasure and luxury, filled with beautiful music, fine food, and sensual perfumes. Jeweled palaces look out onto abundant sweet-smelling flowers and green gardens. A different kind of joy is to be found in the ravishing nymphs, the *apsaras*. The apsaras (which means "moving in the water") are also known as the "wives of the gods" and the "daughters of pleasure": they ensure all happiness and satisfy all passion. They are able to change their form and they bring luck, they enjoy dice and are a reward to heroes who die in battle.

The heaven of the god Indra is situated north of Mount Meru and is known as Svarga, or "Dream." Birds, nymphs, celestial musicians, and beatified mortals live there, as does Kamadhenu, the divine cow which grants all desires. Svarga is famous for Indra's glorious palace, Vaijanta. Wish-fulfilling trees grow in the garden of Nandana that surrounds the palace; the occupants of paradise may sit under the trees and wish for all that they desire. The paradise is scented by the wonderful *parijata* tree, which has golden bark and colorful leaves and is admired by the apsaras.

The paradise of the god Krishna is located at Vrindavan, which is both an earthly city and a divine paradise. Fertile and abundant, Krishna's paradise is named Goloka, the place of cows, and is the home for his devotees, who arrive as cows or other beasts or birds, and as the cowherds and milkmaids (*gopas* and *gopis*) who join Krishna on his moonlit dances of bliss. This dalliance can be seen as a metaphor of the spiritual union between the devotee and the god.

LEFT: Vishnu sleeping upon the coils of the serpent of cosmic time.

THE EDE

VIVIDLY TOLD AT THE BEGINNING OF THE HEBREW BIBLE, JUST TOUCHED UPON IN THE NEW TESTAMENT, THE STORY OF EDEN IS BRILLIANTLY ELABORATED IN THE PAGES OF THE QURAN, WHERE EDEN HAS BECOME PARADISE, A BEAUTIFUL GARDEN SITUATED IN HEAVEN. JEWISH RABBIS CONTINUED TO SPEAK OF EDEN, BUT THEY TOO IMAGINED A HEAVENLY GARDEN OF DELIGHTS. CHRISTIANS MAINTAINED A FIRM BELIEF IN A GARDEN LOCATED ON EARTH; AND A FEW HAD HOPES OF FINDING IT. BUT JESUS HAD SPOKEN OF A HEAVENLY PARADISE ALSO, LEAVING CHRISTIAN THINKERS AND ARTISTS FREE TO SPECULATE: DANTE'S PARADISE IS ABOVE, IN HEAVEN, MILTON'S DOWN BELOW. AMONG NUMBERLESS PORTRAYALS OF PARADISE SOME RETAIN A FLAVOR OF HEAVEN, OTHERS ARE MORE DOWN TO EARTH.

ADAM & EVE

THE KEY TEXT ON THE SUBJECT OF PARADISE—THE STORY IN THE BOOK OF GENESIS OF THE FALL OF ADAM AND EVE AND THEIR EXPULSION FROM THE GARDEN—HAS INSPIRED COUNTLESS PAINTINGS AND SCULPTURES, AT LEAST ONE LITERARY MASTERPIECE, MILTON'S *PARADISE LOST*, AND ONE MUSICAL MASTERPIECE, HAYDN'S *CREATION*.

Chapter

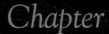

4

For over two millennia scarcely any doubts were cast upon the historical truth of the Genesis account. Nowadays all but a handful of fundamentalists agree that it is a myth. But there agreement ends. What was the location of the garden and its four rivers? Was the fruit really an apple? And, for that matter, was the Fall really a fall? The man called Adam originally had no name at all. And the word "paradise" is missing altogether.

LEFT: The 13th-century mosaic of the Genesis cupola in the basilica of St Mark in Venice portrays the creation and Adam and Eve stories in three concentric rings. Shown here on the right are the creation and blessing of the sea creatures, and on the left Adam's animation (his soul represented as a tiny human figure) and his introduction into paradise.

THE GARDEN OF EDEN

THE BEGINNING

THE FIRST MAN

In the day that the LORD God made the earth and the heavens, when no plant of the field was yet in the earth, and no herb of the field had yet sprung up—for the LORD God had not caused it to rain upon the earth—there was not a man to till the ground. But there went up a mist from the earth, and watered the whole face of the ground. And the LORD God formed man of the dust of the ground, and breathed into his nostrils the breath of life; and man became a living soul.

The Bible opens with an account of the creation of the world in seven days (or rather six, for God rested on the seventh—the Sabbath). This burst of divine activity culminates in the creation, on the sixth day, of man, or rather the human species, both male and female. Yet the second chapter makes it clear that although the earth already exists, it is still empty: a featureless planet, barren, waterless, with no trace of vegetation and nobody to till the soil.

The biblical writer was no less aware than a modern scientist that the one indispensable condition for any form of life, anywhere in the universe, was the presence of water. So the first requirement was irrigation, brought about by a spreading mist or (depending on the translation) by a spring welling up from the ground. Only then did God decide to fashion a human being. The word used, translated here as "fashion," was frequently employed by the biblical writers for the craft of pottery: it carries the sense of careful molding.

Adam, the word for man, is interesting too. We have taken it over as the name of the first man. But originally it meant no more than "human being." (It occurs elsewhere in the Bible as a general term referring to the human race, and is never used in the plural.) The word's intentional resemblance to that for ground or soil, *adamah*, indicates something absolutely fundamental about human nature. The first man was formed out of the very soil he was intended to till. Michelangelo's unforgettable image pictures God rousing Adam into life with, literally, the touch of a finger.

The biblical account is equally striking: an apparently lifeless body being slowly revived by artificial respiration. God himself breathes the breath of life into the first human being. For all his earthy substance, man has something divine about him.

THE GARDEN

And the LORD God planted a garden eastward in Eden; and there he put the man whom he had formed. And out of the ground made the LORD God to grow every tree that is pleasant to the sight, and good for food; the tree of life also in the midst of the garden, and the tree of knowledge of good and evil.

To give this newly-fashioned man somewhere to live God planted a garden. In Hebrew this is just a garden and no more, but when the Bible was translated into Greek for the benefit of Greek-speaking Jews residing in Egyptian Alexandria around 200 B.C.E. the word chosen for garden was *paradeisos*. This had already been introduced into Greek from Persian,

The first evidence of man's despairing search for immortality is found in ancient Mesopotamia, or more precisely in Sumer, and dates back to 3000 B.C.E. *The Epic of Gilgamesh (see also page 14),* which largely concerns the misguided and ultimately futile efforts of its eponymous hero to obtain eternal youth, is without any question the world's oldest literary masterpiece. In the earliest version of the story Gilgamesh is told quite bluntly by the wise goddess Shiduri (who kept an alehouse at the edge of the world):

> *The life that you seek you will never find:*
> *When the gods created mankind,*
> *death they dispensed to mankind,*
> *life they kept for themselves.*

In another version Gilgamesh is told by his friend Uta-napashti (the one human being who had obtained immortality) of a plant at the bottom of the ocean resembling a box-tree. Attaching stones to each of his feet, Gilgamesh dives down and fetches the plant, which he names "Old Man Grown Young," thinking, "I will eat it myself, and be again as I was in my youth!" But the scent of the plant attracts the covetous attentions of a serpent, who steals the plant while Gilgamesh is having a bath, thus ruining his one chance of everlasting youth. Sloughing off its skin, the serpent symbolically enacts the rejuvenation that Gilgamesh himself will never enjoy.

Many of the features of the Garden of Eden story are recognizable here; although the biblical writer articulates them quite differently, his debt to the older tradition is plain.

BELOW: A map of Mesopotamia from a 16th-century Bible.

ABOVE: In Michelangelo's Creation of Adam on the Sistine Chapel ceiling, Adam's alert gaze shows that God is now withdrawing his hand, having already bestowed the gift of life.

LEFT: The East Door of the Florence Baptistery, sculpted in bronze by Lorenzo Ghiberti (1378-1455) is known as the Gate of Paradise. The first panel shows the creation of Adam, the temptation scene in shallower relief just above, the creation of Eve from Adam's sleeping body, and the guilty couple's expulsion from paradise.

where it denoted an estate or park reserved for the exclusive use and enjoyment of kings or princes. The translators evidently felt that the word *paradeisos* would convey more effectively than the standard Greek term for garden the sense they needed of a garden of delights, which it was: the Hebrew name Eden is related linguistically with other words meaning luxury or bliss.

Only two trees are actually named in the garden, and their names indicate immediately that what we are reading is a myth. The Tree of the Knowledge of Good and Evil is at the center of the garden, and indeed at the center of the story. Of the two, it has the more far-reaching consequences for mankind, as the struggle between good and evil is an enduring legacy. The immortality associated with the Tree of Life, on the other hand, has only ever been a dream, or, as here, a tantalizing promise.

Scholars disagree on the precise function of the two trees: it seems likely that the original story had only one, whose fruit contained the knowledge of good and evil. In other words, this was a myth of innocence. Children, unaware of the moral difference between good and evil, are indeed innocent. But humanly speaking their innocence is as much a defect as a virtue. Like them, the first man, though physically mature and fully formed, was still spiritually a child.

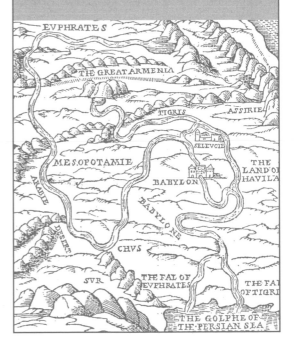

THE OTHER RESIDENTS

THE COMMANDMENT

And the LORD God took the man, and put him into the garden of Eden to dress it and to keep it. And the LORD God commanded the man, saying, Of every tree of the garden thou mayest freely eat. But of the tree of the knowledge of good and evil, thou shalt not eat: for in the day that thou eatest thereof thou shalt surely die.

According to the story the only purpose of the tree in the middle of the garden is to furnish the man with forbidden fruit. Although God might conceivably have tested Adam's mettle by setting him a task to perform—"Climb the tree and gather its fruit"—his very first words take the form of an arbitrary prohibition: "Thou shalt not eat." There have been many interpretations of this incident, including that of Sigmund Freud, who saw God as a projection of one of the three divisions of the human psyche, the so-called super-ego,

which busies itself ordering around the conscious self, the ego. Equally puzzling is the terrible punishment assigned to this seemingly trivial offense: what a lot of fuss about an apple! A little further on in the Bible really serious crimes are committed. Cain murders his brother Abel out of envy, and shortly afterward there is an upsurge of violence that results in a deluge (the Flood). But what kind of God imposes a death sentence for eating an apple? Could his only motive for not allowing Adam to eat the fruit be his determination to keep the knowledge of good and evil to himself? And in that case, why put the tree in the garden in the first place? The point where the story takes off is also the start of all the puzzles. Are we reading it right, or somehow taking it more seriously than was meant?

The huge wheel of tradition, revolving inexorably for nearly two millennia, informs in the Christian reader an understanding of the story, whether consciously or not, in the context of what theologians call Original Sin. It is assumed from the outset that this is a tragedy, probably the greatest tragedy ever to have befallen the human race. But what if it is not a tragedy at all? Suppose that instead of turning to Milton for an understanding of this story one turns to Aesop or La Fontaine, to Hilaire Belloc or Roald Dahl. Bear in mind that the terrible sentence imposed by God was not actually carried out. The day Adam ate the fruit was not the day he died. The punishment God inflicted on him was the normal lot of humanity. There is some advantage in thinking of this story as, above all else, a cautionary tale. Don't mess with authority.

THE BEASTS AND THE BIRDS

And the LORD God said, It is not good that the man should be alone; I will make him an help meet for him. And out of the ground the LORD God formed every beast of the field, and every fowl of the air; and brought them unto Adam to see what he would call them: and whatsoever Adam called every living creature, that was the name thereof. And Adam gave names to all cattle, and to the fowl of the air, and to every beast of the field; but for Adam there was not found an help meet for him.

The first chapter of Genesis recounts how the chaos that was there before the creation was transformed into cosmos, disorder into order. This was done by separating light from darkness, dry land from the ocean, and so on. In this passage God's work of separation— or discrimination—is pursued: the birds are distinguished from the beasts, and the cattle are distinguished from other "beasts of the field." The word translated "cattle" is a general term for farm animals, better suited than

The Tree of Life

A bi-lingual (Sumerian/Akkadian) text speaks of a tree called *giškin/kiškanû* with magical healing powers, growing in the fertile domain of Eridu, between "the river of two mouths," probably the confluence of the Tigris and the Euphrates on the Persian Gulf. The tree, rooted in the apsû, the ocean residence of the kindly god Ea (Sumerian Enki), has the appearance of lapiz lazuli, is inaccessible to humans, but frequented by the sun god Shamash, and the sovereign of heaven, Tammuz.

The oldest images of this tree depict it as a cult-symbol. A series of Assyrian cylindrical seals show priestly figures in fish-skins carrying a pail of lustral water in one hand and lifting the other in a gesture of adoration, the god usually occupying the center of a solar disk above the sacred tree. One seal portrays a blossoming tree on top of a mountain, while from a winged disk in the sky above two outstretched hands pour water into vases at the foot of the mountain.

In a general way, the tree of life was thought to be rooted in the underworld with a trunk passing through the center of the earth and branches that reached up to the sky and supported the stars. Perhaps the finest expression of this motif in the Jewish tradition is in Nebuchadnezzar's dream in the Book of Daniel: "I saw, and behold, a tree in the midst of the earth; and its height was great. The tree grew and became strong, and its top reached to heaven, and it was visible to the end of the whole earth. Its leaves were fair and its fruit abundant, and in it was food for all. The beasts of the field found shade under it, and the birds of the air dwelt in its branches, and all flesh was fed from it."

ABOVE: This 13th-century pulpit in Ferrara Cathedral shows how the motif of the tree of life was interpreted in a society dependent on the grape harvest for its existence.

the others for lending Adam a helping hand; but we have to remember that this is still paradise, and Adam has not yet been told that he must till the soil from which he has been fashioned.

That Adam names the beasts is also significant. In many primitive societies the act of conferring a name is thought to carry with it power and authority. This is plainly an anthropocentric universe, although there is no hint yet of any right to hunt or even to corral "the beasts of the field." Yet the man is clearly in charge.

THE FIRST WOMAN

And the LORD God caused a deep sleep to fall upon Adam, and he slept: and he took one his ribs, and closed up the flesh instead thereof. And the rib, which the LORD God had taken from man, made he a woman, and brought her unto the man. And Adam said, This is now bone of my bones, and flesh of my flesh: she shall be called Woman, because she was taken out of Man. Therefore shall a man leave his father and his mother, and shall cleave unto his wife: and they shall be one flesh. And they were both naked, the man and his wife, and were not ashamed.

From a woman's point of view the implications of this story appear entirely negative. It is unquestionably the product of a male-centered world, and the three main heirs of this tradition—Judaism, Christianity, and Islam—have on the whole retained the concept of the inherent priority and superiority of the male, with profound consequences that still reverberate today. Yet the story has positive implications too. The woman, as Adam acknowledges, is truly bone of his bones and flesh of his flesh, a proper mate and companion.

Scholars disagree about whether the couple had sexual relations while still in the garden. Christian tradition overwhelmingly takes the view that they did not; but the text does speak of the pair as "one flesh." What is clear is that, in their state of childlike innocence, they felt no embarrassment at being naked.

BELOW: In his 16th-century woodcut Gregor Reisch depicts a key moment in the story: God creates the first woman, Eve, from Adam's rib.

LEFT: *Like his medieval predecessors, Martin Luther's friend and portraitist Lucas Cranach shows the different scenes of the paradise story in a single painting. Wild and domestic animals (and even the legendary unicorn) are shown lying peacefully side by side.*

THE ACT

THE SERPENT

Now the serpent was more subtil than any beast of the field which the LORD God had made. And he said unto the woman, Yea, hath God said, Ye shall not eat of every tree of the garden? And the woman said unto the serpent, We may eat of the fruit of the trees of the garden: but of the fruit of the tree which is in the midst of the garden, God hath said, Ye shall not eat of it, neither shall ye touch it, lest ye die. And the serpent said unto the woman, Ye shall not surely die. For God doth know that in the day ye eat thereof, then your eyes shall be opened, and ye shall be as gods, knowing good and evil.

Not many people like snakes, and the serpent in Eden has received few favorable notices. The Hebrew word used to describe him (for he is clearly a male), 'arum, can have a negative connotation (crafty, cunning) or a positive one (shrewd, prudent). Subtil (= subtle) is not a bad translation, placing the serpent among a group of animals like the fox or the ant that might in a moral tale exemplify cleverness.

The word 'arum resembles the word for naked ('arummim) used in the preceding verse. The ironic contrast between the defenselessness of the human couple and the resourcefulness of the serpent is emphasized. Approaching the woman (not slithering, for he can still walk) the serpent counters God's injunction not to eat the fruit of the tree by telling her: "You will not die." There is ambiguity here. If he was alluding to God's threat of immediate punishment—death that very day—then he was telling the truth. (Adam is supposed to have lived to the age of 930.) His promise that she would know good and evil was equally true. "Your eyes will be opened." They were.

According to the ancient myth used by the biblical writer as the basis of his story, the knowledge of good and evil was bestowed on humanity as a gift. Did the serpent, then, help to pass on this gift, in a manner reminiscent of the generous act of the Titan Prometheus in a parallel Greek myth, who incurred the malignant fury of Zeus. by bringing fire to mankind? This is an alternative way of looking at the story.

DISOBEDIENCE

And when the woman saw that the tree was good for food, and that it was pleasant to the eyes, and a tree to be desired to make one wise, she took of the fruit thereof, and did eat, and gave also unto her husband with her; and he did eat. And the eyes of them both were opened, and they knew that they were naked; and they sewed fig-leaves together, and made themselves aprons.

This is the crucial episode, the fateful act. The terms sin, guilt, transgression and—most notably—fall are absent from the story itself, and nowhere in the Hebrew Bible is it stated or even suggested that Adam and Eve were responsible for the entry of sin and death into the world. That inference was drawn much later. But it is not the only possible reading. Many people, beginning with the author of the so-called Hypostasis of the Archons in the second century C.E., have thought that the acquisition of the knowledge of good and evil was a prize that more than compensated for the punishment that followed. According to this Gnostic text the serpent is, so to speak, on the side of the angels, and the real villain of the piece is the Jewish God, enviously denying to man the knowledge that is rightfully his. Much later the philosopher Kant, whose motto *sapere aude* means "dare to know," thought of the Fall as a step forward, not backward.

There is nothing to suggest that either the man or the woman was prompted by pride or envy when reaching for the fruit. There was nothing wrong with the tree itself or the fruit that it provided, "good for food and a delight to the eyes," or indeed with the wisdom that could be acquired by eating it. And if the consequence of their action was that their eyes were opened it is hard to see what was wrong with that either.

What then does account for our instinctively negative interpretation? The first use of the word "fall" to describe the event comes in a Jewish work known as *4 Ezra*, towards the end of the first century C.E.: "O Adam, what have you done? For though it was you who sinned, the fall was not yours alone, but ours also who are your descendants. For what good is it that an everlasting hope has been promised to us, but we have done deeds that bring death?"

The word was also used by the Christian Hippolytus of Rome a century or so later, and it has subsequently become the standard shorthand description of the episode in Western art and literature.

The truth is, however, that the origins of our negative reading lie much earlier. The Jewish Ben Sira, who wrote around the beginning of the second century B.C.E., takes a very sour view of womankind (though he is not alone in this): "For from garments comes the moth, and from a woman comes woman's wickedness. Better is the wickedness of a man than a woman who does good; and it is a woman who brings shame and disgrace." His verdict on Eve is particularly uncompromising: "From a woman sin had its beginning and because of her we all die." Sometimes this tendency is taken to the point of exonerating Adam altogether. Did he fall, or was he pushed? Saint Paul, for instance, or someone writing in his name to his disciple Timothy, betrays manifest bias: "For Adam was formed first, then Eve; and Adam was not deceived, but the woman was deceived and became a transgressor."

CONFRONTATION

And they heard the voice of the LORD God walking in the garden in the cool of the day: and Adam and his wife hid themselves from the presence of the LORD God amongst the trees of the garden. And the LORD God called unto Adam, and said unto him, Where art thou? And he said, I heard thy voice in the garden, and I was afraid, because I was naked; and I hid myself. And he said, Who told thee that thou wast naked? Hast thou eaten of the tree, whereof I commanded thee that thou shouldest not eat? And the man said, The woman whom thou gavest to be with me, she gave me of the tree, and I did eat. And the LORD God said unto the woman, What is this that thou hast done? And the woman said, The serpent beguiled me, and I did eat.

Naturally God confronts the man first. The man blames the woman and the woman blames the serpent. They both respond for all the world like naughty children.

BELOW: In Albrecht Dürer's early 16th-century painting of Eve, Eve has eaten one apple, and now holds another that she is about to offer Adam, looking at him nervously but also challengingly.

THE CURSE

THE SERPENT

*And the LORD God said unto the serpent, Because
thou hast done this, thou art cursed above all cattle, and
above every beast of the field; upon thy belly shalt thou
go, and dust shalt thou eat all the days of thy life. And I
will put enmity between thee and the woman, and
between thy seed and her seed; it shall bruise thy head,
and thou shalt bruise his heel.*

Why do snakes crawl or slide instead of walking
upright or on all fours like other animals? Scientists
will answer in terms of evolutionary theory, knowing
that snakes are descended from lizards and possess ves-
tigal legbones; but what we have here is an alternative
way of responding to questions like this one, with an
etiological, or explanatory, myth.

Up to this point the serpent had been classed
among "the beasts of the field." Now, condemned out
of hand with no chance to defend himself, he is put in
a category of his own, outlawed from both field and
farm. Much of the curse concerns the serpent's "seed,"
rendered in modern translations as "offspring." The
(masculine) Hebrew word for seed refers to the entire
progeny of a person (or, in this case, of an animal). The
Greek word used to translate it, *sperma*, is neuter, but

the pronoun referring back to it, *autos*, is masculine.
There is no reason to suppose that the translators had
anything other in mind than a representative serpent
who had inherited the curse. Nevertheless the masculine pronoun opens the way for the interpretation of *the
woman's seed*, as well as the serpent's, as a single individual. So starting with Irenaeus, Bishop of Lyons in
the second century, Christian writers have interpreted
the woman's seed as Christ, and later the woman herself as Mary the mother of Jesus.

The progeny of the serpent too came to be thought
of in some circles as a single individual; and in the Book
of Revelation, which concludes the Christian Bible, he
is already identified as Satan, the great deceiver. There
can be few better proofs of the immense significance
carried by a grammatical oddity, for had the author of
Revelation read this story in Hebrew rather than Greek
he could never have come to make this connection.

THE WOMAN

*Unto the woman he said, I will greatly multiply thy sor-
row and thy conception; in sorrow thou shalt bring forth
children; and thy desire shall be to thy husband, and he
shall rule over thee.*

The affliction that women often speak of as the curse is
not included among the punishments listed here. But it

ABOVE: *In this fresco on
the ceiling of the Sistine
Chapel does Michelangelo
betray a certain misogyny in
depicting the serpent (whose
lower half is coiled round the
tree) with a woman's breasts?*

might well have received a mention because here is another example of mythical etiology, a story told to account for features of human and animal life that provoke puzzlement and curiosity.

Today, when all but the irredeemably stupid readily acknowledge the fundamental equality of men and women, it is hard to read this part of the story without some sense of shock. Startling as we may find the uncompromising assertion of the woman's subjection to the man, we should remember that it was made at a time and from within a society that never questioned the right of husbands to demand obedience from their wives. In fairness, the depiction of the woman in the story as a whole is far from unattractive. Her character is strong: it is she who takes the initiative and, for reasons that seem far from disreputable, decides to eat the fruit. The use made of the story in later traditions, both Jewish and Christian, is a distortion of the original picture.

THE MAN

And unto Adam he said, Because thou hast hearkened unto the voice of thy wife, and hast eaten of the tree, of which I commanded thee, saying, Thou shalt not eat of it: cursed is the ground for thy sake; in sorrow shalt thou eat of it all the days of thy life. Thorns also and thistles shall it bring forth to thee; and thou shalt eat the herb of the field. In the sweat of thy face shalt thou eat bread, till thou return unto the ground; for out of it wast thou taken: for dust thou art, and unto dust shalt thou return.

Here are answers to another series of puzzles: why men have to toil all their days to make a living, why the soil is so often inhospitable, and why a man's life, like that of his wife, is so all-pervasively burdensome.

By heaping the blame for these miseries on the disobedient pair themselves, the author is suggesting that no blame is to be attached to God. But the result, however unintentional, is that he puts God in the same unflattering, self-exculpating light as the couple he has just condemned. It's all your fault, God seems to be saying, not mine: you brought all these troubles on yourselves, so don't hold me responsible.

Worse than this, in reproaching the man for listening to his wife the God of the story invites future readers to lay the blame for all the woes of the world on the woman. However muted, the misogyny is recognizable, and later writers, both Jewish and Christian, were quick to exploit it.

The concluding words of the curse look like a death sentence. After a long and arduous life the man will eventually return to the dust (or clay) from which he was originally fashioned. But this fate is not part of the

curse. The sentence imposed upon the man for his disobedience is not death but life: a life of hard labor. From a literary point of view this conclusion is also an inclusion, that is to say a way of rounding off the story by referring back, often by repeating the same words, to its beginning. That Adam should eventually return to the *adamah* (soil or earth) from which he first came and which he is now going to have to till is a natural and—from the author's perspective—a satisfactory end to a well-told tale.

The Battle of the Stars

*T*hematically linked with the story of Lucifer's fall is the part he played in the battle of the stars, the concluding episode of Book V of the *Sibylline Oracles*, a product of Egyptian Judaism composed in Greek toward the beginning of the second century C.E.

*"I saw the threat of the burning sun among the stars
and the terrible wrath of the moon among the lightning flashes.
The stars travailed in battle; God bade them fight.
For over against the sun long flames were in strife,
And the two-horned rush of the moon was changed.
Lucifer fought, mounted on the back of Leo.
Capricorn smote the ankle of the young Taurus,
and Taurus deprived Capricorn of his day of return.
Orion removed Libra so that it remained no more.
Virgo changed the destiny of Gemini in Aries.
The Pleiad no longer appeared and Draco rejected its belt.
Cancer did not stand its ground, for it feared Orion.
Scorpio hid beneath its tail because of terrible Leo,
and the dog star perished by the flame of the sun.
The strength of the mighty day star burned up Aquarius.
Heaven itself was roused until it shook the fighters.
In anger it cast them headlong to earth.
Accordingly, stricken into the baths of ocean,
they quickly kindled the whole earth. But the sky remained starless."*

ABOVE: A 16th-century fresco by Giovanni De Vecchi and Raffaellino da Reggio on the ceiling of the Sala del Mappamondo in the Farnese palace in Rome, showing the constellations.

EXPULSION

A NAME FOR THE WOMAN

And Adam called his wife's name Eve; because she was the mother of all living. Unto Adam also and to his wife did the LORD God make coats of skins, and clothed them.

These verses form the beginning of what can be regarded as an appendix to the story, which rounds it off by adding a few finishing touches.

The name the man now gives his wife is the first proper name, unless we count God himself, to occur in the Hebrew Bible. Adam, as we have seen, is just a generic term for a human being. Eve is a name, a marvellous name too, for it proclaims her to be "the mother of all living." (The Hebrew for Eve, *chawwah*, resembles *chayyah*: living thing or life.)

The story is a fable, one whose general relevance to the human condition the author does not attempt to disguise. But within the story itself the allusions to the experience of the race and, equally significantly, of the reader are at best hints and guesses. But as he ends his story the author moves outside it, and simply by pointing to the derivation of Eve's name flings open the window to the life of the entire universe then and now: she is the mother of all living.

The naming of Eve is Adam's last act. Immediately afterward God shows for the first time a touch of solicitousness for his human creatures. Within the story they covered their nakedness and concealed their embarrassment with makeshift aprons or loin-cloths made of hastily stitched fig-leaves. Now this strangely enigmatic God replaces these with leather garments of his own design. The progress from frank and unembarrassed nakedness to the kind of helpless dismay that often accompanies a sudden awareness of nakedness is surely significant. Equally so is the contrast between the couple's own furtive, pathetic attempts to cover their nakedness with a few leaves and God's determination to provide them with proper clothing. This can be seen as a recognition that the pair were about to abandon forever the childish state of blissful innocence in which nakedness could be ignored, and to move into a recognizably human society where it is taken for granted that people wear clothes.

IMMORTALITY LOST

And the LORD God said, Behold, the man is become as one of us, to know good and evil: and now, lest he put forth his hand, and take also of the tree of life, and eat, and live for ever. Therefore the LORD God sent him forth from the garden of Eden, to till the ground from whence he was taken.

"Like one of us": suddenly the deity has multiplied. In fact the word for God, *Elohim*, has a plural form, and although it is generally treated as a grammatical singular, from time to time it crops up in contexts where it has to be translated as "gods." Usually the biblical writers resist or deliberately gloss over any hint that there may be other deities with rival claims on men's allegiance. But here, as in the conclusion to the first chapter, at the point where the decision is taken to create man, the creator is portrayed as entering into

LEFT AND FAR LEFT: *Details from* The Story of Adam and Eve *by Giovanni Boccaccio (1313-75). In the picture on the far left the angel cherubim set to guard the gate of paradise with a sword is here, as often, shown carrying out the expulsion. In the picture on the near left depicting hard labor, Adam has a difficult job digging the soil. Eve, surrounded by animals, is spinning, traditionally a woman's task.*

consultation with his fellow gods: "Let us make man in our image, after our likeness."

The desired resemblance cannot be achieved until the man has acquired the knowledge of good and evil. What was a privilege strictly reserved for the divinity has now become a necessary characteristic of the adult human being.

Why do we lament the fall of man? Franz Kafka sums it up accurately enough: "We were not driven out of Paradise because of the tree of the knowledge of good and evil; but because of the tree of life, that we might not eat of it." Though we speak of lost immortality, the fruit of the tree of life had never actually been sampled. If it had, and if the life it contained had included the gift of eternal youthfulness, then Adam and Eve would have been truly like gods. But this prospect was never more than a distant dream; God was never going to allow it.

EXCLUSION

So he drove out the man; and he placed at the east of the garden of Eden Cherubims, and a flaming sword which turned every way, to keep the way of the tree of life.

Cherubim is simply the Hebrew plural of the word *cherub*, but these cherubim are anything but cherubic. The chubby winged boys, or putti, that crowd the ceilings of baroque churches are the linear descendants of the angelic order of cherubim, whose sole function was to sing God's praises; but this was not how they began. Originally they were therianthropes, half-human, half-animal creatures like centaurs or mermaids. In Assyria, from where the Jews borrowed them, they were winged bulls or lions with human features who guarded the king's palace. In a subsequent chapter we shall see that Israel was to give the cherubim another important role to play.

ABOVE: *The chubby cherubs of later Christian art have little in common, apart from their residual wings, with the powerful cherubim of the Bible who are their distant ancestors.*

OTHER FALLS

THE KING OF TYRE

This story is an alternative (and probably earlier) version of the fall and expulsion of the first man from the Garden of Eden.

The King of Tyre, who figures in one of Ezekiel's prophecies, is said to have inhabited the Garden of Eden and is described as "full of wisdom and perfect in beauty." Although he differs from Adam in all sorts of ways—he is a king, for instance, and already endowed with wisdom—the King of Tyre is clearly a close relative.

The text speaks of a multiplicity of jewels, including sapphires and emeralds, that serve as a "covering" for the king, perhaps a fantastically ornate piece of clothing comparable to the breastplate or pectoral worn by the high priest, so the Greek translators inferred that the king was also a priest. It has even been suggested that this garden, which was located on top of a mountain, is to be identified with the Jewish temple, and that the rituals presided over by the priest-king reflected the workings of the heavenly council of God.

There is also mention of a guardian cherub who, rather than keeping watch at the gate of Eden in order to prevent Adam's return (as in the Genesis version), is positioned here to protect the king.

"What is man," cries the Psalmist to God, "or the son of man (*ben adam*) that thou art mindful of him? Yet thou hast made him little less than God (or the gods), and dost crown him with glory and honor." This quotation, applied by the very earliest Christian writers to Christ himself, was almost certainly first addressed to primal man, a splendid royal figure like the King of Tyre, and it shows how pervasive this myth had become, being found in each of the three great divisions of the Bible, the law (Genesis), the prophets (Ezekiel), and the writings (Psalms). Though created perfect in mind and body, of incomparable wisdom and beauty, this ideal figure soon fell prey to moral corruption: "By the multitude of your iniquities, in the unrighteousness of your trade you profaned your sanctuaries."

The king's end was far worse than Adam's. The guardian cherub appointed to watch over the king drove him out of the garden, and God pronounced a terrible sentence: "I brought forth fire from the midst of you; it consumed you, and I turned you to ashes upon the earth in the sight of all who saw you. All who know you among the peoples are appalled at you; you have come to a dreadful end and shall be no more for ever."

LUCIFER

Strikingly similar to the fall of the King of Tyre is Isaiah's account of the fall of the King of Babylon. This villainous prince is described as an angel, and specifically identified with the Day Star, son of Dawn, otherwise known as Lucifer, the bringer of light: "You said in your heart, 'I will ascend to heaven; above the stars of God I will set my throne on high; I will sit on the mount of assembly in the far north; I will ascend above the heights of the clouds; I will make myself like the Most High.' But you are brought down to Sheol, to the depths of the Pit."

The offense of this angel-king far exceeded that of Adam, even though he and Eve were invited by the serpent to believe that the knowledge of good and evil would make them God's equal. But whatever the offense, whether the comparatively trivial matter of sampling forbidden fruit or the heinous crime of *lèse-majesté*, the Bible insists throughout that the fundamental sin is that of disobedience.

OPPOSITE: The Fall of the Rebel Angels by Jean-Marc Nattier (1685-1766), one of numerous paintings with this title, offers a vivid depiction of a story told in a variety of ways by many writers, both Jewish and Christian.

BELOW: This elaborately jewelled crown may evoke the fantastically ornate clothing worn by the King of Tyre.

THE FALL OF SATAN

One memorable scene that has come to be associated with the story of Adam and Eve reverses the ascension story by telling instead of the disgrace of the rebel angels and their fall into Hell.

The Book of Genesis merely hints at this terrible event with an obscure allusion to "the sons of God" (angels) who aroused God's anger by consorting with the daughters of men. But the *Life of Adam and Eve* brings the connection into focus by making Satan complain that the loss of his glorious place among the angels was entirely Adam's fault. Adam is puzzled, so Satan tells him that after God had breathed life into him he was immediately conducted (by Michael) into the presence of God and his angels, who were then ordered to worship him: "Here is Adam," God said, "I have made him in our image and likeness."

Michael repeats God's command over and over again, to no avail. "I will not worship an inferior and younger being," Satan declares. "I am his senior in creation. I was made before him, and he ought to worship me." The certainty of imminent punishment fails to move him: "If God is angry with me I will take my seat above the stars of heaven and I will be like the Most High." (Just like Lucifer, the Day Star, in Isaiah.)

For this act of defiance Satan, along with his fellow rebels, is banished for ever from the divine court. He tells Adam that in his misery and fury at seeing him enjoying an easy life in paradise, "I beguiled your wife and used her to have you driven from your joy and luxury, just as I was driven from my glory."

The punishment of the rebel angels is told more dramatically in I Enoch. It begins, like Genesis, with the report that rebel angels (or "giants") consorted with "the daughters of men." The result was that the women "gave birth to giants to the degree that the whole earth was filled with blood and oppression." Another angel, Raphael, was told to bind Azazel hand and foot (Azazel is Enoch's name for the rebel leader, who had committed all sorts of other crimes as well), and to throw him into darkness: "And he made a hole in the desert and cast him there; he threw rugged and sharp rocks on top of him. And he covered his face to prevent him from seeing the light and in order that he might be sent into the fire on the great day of judgment."

From a historical point of view the most important account is the first brief mention of the

ABOVE: *Gustave Doré (1823-83) furnished illustrations for the Bible, Dante, and Milton. This picture illustrates the end of Book 3 of* Paradise Lost *where Milton describes how Satan reaches paradise, as:*
    Toward the coast of earth beneath,
    Down from the ecliptic, sped with hoped success,
    [He] throws his steep flight in many an airy wheel.

OPPOSITE: *Domenico Beccafumi (1484-1551). The Fall of the Rebel Angels. As often, the archangel Michael, sword in hand, presides over the expulsion of the rebel angels from heaven.*

story in the Christian Book of Revelation, the only place in the whole Bible in which Satan is explicitly identified with the serpent that tempted Eve: "And the great dragon was cast out, that old serpent, called the Devil, and Satan, which deceiveth the whole world: he was cast out into the earth, and his angels were cast out with him."

THE JEWISH PARADISE

LONG BEFORE THE ARRIVAL OF CHRISTIANITY THE NOTION OF PARADISE HAD BEGUN TO CHANGE. THE GATE TO THE GARDEN OF EARTHLY DELIGHTS SEEMED TO BE PERMANENTLY BARRED. BUT THE LONGING FOR IMMORTALITY ENSHRINED IN THE MYTH DID NOT GO AWAY, AND A NEW IDEA GRADUALLY TOOK SHAPE OF A PARADISE IN THE SKY.

Chapter 5

This heavenly garden had already been visited by certain chosen souls, believed to have been transported up to the heavens in dreams or visions, and this belief was one of the sources of a mystical tradition that persisted in Judaism well into the common era.

LEFT: The Vision of the Prophet Ezekiel by Raphael (Raphael Sanzio), (1483–1520). Raphael interprets as cherubs the cherubim (winged creatures) who form the throne-chariot of God. The cherubim have four faces, but only the eagle is seen here. Ezekiel's vision is the origin of the long Jewish tradition known as merkabah mysticism.

PARADISE LOST

The Bible furnishes only limited information about developing concepts of life after death. To understand how and why notions of paradise came to change we must turn to a huge number of diverse Jewish and Christian documents more or less contemporary with the Bible.

Our principal sources are found in two large groups of writings: the Old Testament apocrypha—a great number of works of varying lengths and genres that hover on the edge of the Bible but were never formally admitted into the canon—and the pseudepigrapha, pseudonymous texts attributed to a range of biblical characters from the familiar, like Abraham, to the less well known, such as Baruch, amanuensis of the prophet Jeremiah. Many of the writings in both categories are either of Christian provenance or else have been expanded by their Christian editors. All, with only a couple of very late exceptions, have come down to us through Christian channels. The Jewish rabbis were confident that God's entire revelation was contained in the Bible (the written tradition) or else in the oral traditions of rabbinical teachings gathered together in the Mishnah, published around 200 B.C.E. (The Mishnah has the same kind of authority for believing Jews as the New Testament has for Christians.) The rabbis wanted nothing to do with the purported additions to the revealed word of God in the apocrypha and pseudepigrapha.

Yet from the scholar's point of view these writings are no less valuable than the Bible itself for the evidence they afford of the beliefs and practices prevalent at the time and place of their composition. The same is true of the other sources available, especially the Dead Sea Scrolls (discovered in 1947 but only published in their entirety in the last decade of the twentieth century) and the copious writings of the historian Josephus and the philosopher Philo. Although both of these authors were Jewish their works would have been lost to view had they not been handed down to posterity by interested Christians.

ADAM AND EVE

EARTHLY PARADISE

Astonishingly, in view of the dramatic and colorful commencement of the Book of Genesis, the Hebrew Bible turns its back almost immediately upon Adam and Eve, and their story receives no further mention in its pages. If we had to rely on the Bible alone for our knowledge of Jewish beliefs and customs we should be forced to conclude that Israel had lost all interest in this fascinating myth. But fortunately that is not the case. The apocryphal *Life of Adam and Eve* makes it clear that—at least in some circles—Jewish belief in the continuing existence and relevance of the Garden of Eden persisted well into the common era. This writing (which also survives in a rather longer Greek version called, puzzlingly, *The Apocalypse of Moses*), is the work of a Jewish author roughly contemporary with Saint Paul.

It pictures Adam and Eve shut out of Paradise and bemoaning their lot. Where the Genesis account has the serpent as the only real villain, the newer story casts the serpent in a subordinate role as the tool of Satan. Modern readers may find it hard to credit that a fable of this kind can ever have been read as a true account of events that actually occurred in history. But this, like all the other apocrypha, was attached to the Bible because it was believed to have been inspired by God; and it is this belief that accounts for its survival.

After being thrown out of Paradise Adam and Eve wander around disconsolately for the best part of a month eating nothing but grass. Eve proposes to Adam that since she was the one responsible for their plight he should take her life. Horrified at this suggestion, he urges instead genuine repentance—"perhaps the Lord God will be gracious to us and pity us and give us something to live on"—and decides to embark on a 40-day fast. He commands Eve to go to the river Tigris and stand on a stone, silent and motionless, with the water up to her neck, for 37 days (a few days less than Adam because he recognizes that she is not as strong as he is). Adam takes himself to the river Jordan, where he too stands fasting in the water. All the living creatures in the river grieve along with him and the waters stop flowing.

Enter Satan. Seeing Eve in the Tigris, he urges her to leave the river and take some food, using the same kind of argument as the serpent in Genesis. Eve proves to be just as gullible as before. Emerging from the river, her body is "blue with cold" and she collapses. Rebuked by Adam for succumbing yet again to the devil's wiles, "she fell on her face on the earth, and her sorrow and groaning and wailing were redoubled."

OPPOSITE: The fragmentary parchment manuscripts known as The Dead Sea Scrolls discovered in 1947 at Qumran, on the western shore of the Dead Sea, are an important source of information about Judaism at the turn of the era.

FAR RIGHT: Bartolomé Bermejo (worked between 1474-95) shows Saint Michael trampling on the defeated Satan, depicted as a dragon.

Adam too is tempted by Satan but resists his blandishments and continues his fast, remaining up to his neck in the Jordan for the full 40 days. (Adam was steadfast where Eve was weak—further proof of the enduring tendency to shift all the blame onto the woman.)

The story proceeds with the birth of the couple's children. When Adam dies, surrounded by his 63 children, at the age of 930, God commands his body to be carried ceremoniously to the outskirts of Paradise, preceded by a procession of angels. There he is buried alongside his son Abel by the angels Michael and Uriel. Eve dies a week later.

HEAVENLY PARADISE

This story (and there are others) demonstrates the persistence within Judaism of the memory of Eden. Implicit in it is the conviction that paradise still existed somewhere on the earth, distant and inaccessible but still an object of nostalgia and desire. At the same time there was another very different way of conceiving paradise, not as a garden of earthly delights but as a region outside and above the earth. This notion makes its appearance in stories of heavenly ascents, and one such episode is included in the apocryphal *Life of Adam and Eve*. Adam tells his son Seth that, while he and Eve were at prayer,

"Michael the archangel, a messenger of God, came to me. And I saw a chariot like the wind, and its wheels were fiery; and I was caught up into the Paradise of righteousness. And I saw the Lord sitting; and his face was a burning fire that no man could endure."

Elsewhere the heavenly paradise appears as a resting place, either a temporary stopover where chosen souls could await the day of judgment, or a permanent home.

THE DIVINE CHARIOT

ENOCH'S JOURNEY

According to Jewish tradition the first person to ascend to heaven so as to walk with God was the patriarch Enoch, a descendant of Adam's third son, Seth: "Enoch walked with God; and he was not, for God took him." This brief and enigmatic report generated a remarkably wide body of Jewish literature. How did Enoch suddenly cease to be? Because God took him. And how did he walk with God? The inference was drawn that Enoch was transported to a place where he could see God and behold his glorious dwelling-place. This idea gave rise to speculations that found expression in no fewer than three apocryphal Books of Enoch. The oldest of the three Books of Enoch (1 Enoch, sometimes called Ethiopian Enoch) was unknown in the West apart from a few extracts until the end of the eighteenth century, when the explorer James Bruce brought back a manuscript from Abyssinia (now Ethiopia). This was translated and published in 1821 (soon enough to have been read by William Blake, who died in 1827) as The Book of Enoch the

BELOW LEFT: A fresco from the church of Santa Maria de Tahull in Spain by a 12th-century Romanesque artist shows the weighing of souls at the last judgment. The idea that souls could be weighed after death to determine the relative amount of good and evil practiced during their lives was popular in the Middle Ages, and is illustrated in many miniatures and church wall paintings.

Prophet. Later in the century a number of Greek fragments were discovered, and in the middle of the twentieth century other significant but much smaller Aramaic fragments were found at Qumran. It is a composite work, but parts of it, including the one that concerns us here (The Book of Watchers), are very old, dating back at least as far as the third century B.C.E. What follows is an abbreviated account of Enoch's vision in chapter 14 of this book.

After being called by clouds and mist, harried by flashes of lightning, and lifted up by winds so that he felt himself to be flying, Enoch reaches a house constructed of marble:

"And I entered that house, and it was hot as fire and cold as snow, and there was neither pleasure nor life in it. Fear covered me and trembling took hold of me."

He sees an open door leading into a second, larger and more magnificent house, with a fiery floor and a fiery roof, which gives him more satisfaction. On entering it he says,

"I saw in it a lofty throne, and its appearance was like crystal and its wheels like the shining sun... And from underneath the lofty throne there flowed out rivers of burning fire so that it was impossible to look at it. And he who is great in glory sat on it, and his raiment was brighter than the sun, and whiter than any snow... A sea of fire burnt around him and a great fire stood before him, and none of those around him came near to him."

Many of the features of Enoch's vision recur in the Book of Revelation, and although paradise is not specifically mentioned, Eden is not far away. The two houses, one leading to the other by an open door, probably represent the two courts, outer and inner, of the

Jerusalem temple. In a later vision in the same part of the book Enoch visits a place of seven mountains, among them a tree of extraordinary beauty: "Beautiful to look at and pleasant are its leaves, and its fruit very delightful in appearance." He is told by the angel Michael that "from its fruit life will be given to the chosen" and that "towards the north it will be planted, in a holy place, by the house of the Lord, the Eternal King." This, then, is the tree of life. It is still on earth, as Enoch emphasizes, but points unmistakably to heaven.

EZEKIEL'S VISION

One puzzling feature in the account of Enoch's heavenly journey is the reference to the wheels of the throne he saw in the second mansion. The appearance of this "chariot throne" and the mention of wheels places Enoch's vision firmly in the category of what came to be called merkabah mysticism. The word merkabah means chariot, and the term "merkabah mysticism" refers to one of the two main branches of Jewish mysticism, based on the contemplation of the first chapter of the Book of Ezekiel.

The visionary experience of Ezekiel, like that of Enoch, began in a storm (clouds and lightning are specifically mentioned), but before seeing the divine throne he witnesses the strange sight of four living creatures, each of them somehow associated with a wheel. The wheels have spokes, "and their rims were full of eyes round about." Each of the creatures has four faces, one like a lion, another like an ox, the third like a man and the fourth like an eagle. (These were later to be adopted as the symbols of the four evangelists.) Above the heads of the living creatures the prophet describes a firmament (the term for that part of the sky which was thought to separate earth from heaven) "shining like crystal"—resembling in this respect the throne in Enoch's vision. Above the firmament is a throne, and "seated above the likeness of a throne was a likeness as it were of a human form." Despite his misgivings (evident from this hesitant beginning) the prophet goes on to describe the figure seated on the throne: it is, without any question, God himself.

Not all the elements of the divine chariot are yet present, for not only is the word "chariot" missing, but it is clear that the vision of the divine throne followed

the vision of the wheels. But in another vision in the same book the living creatures, now identified as cherubim, act as a kind of throne for "the glory of the Lord." And another biblical book, 1 Chronicles, recounts how in the instructions he gave to his son Solomon concerning the construction of the temple, King David included his "plan for the golden chariot of the cherubim that spread their wings and covered the ark of the covenant of the Lord." This instruction takes us into the heart of the temple, the Holy of Holies, and the site of the ark of the covenant. Not surprisingly, many of the descriptions of heaven prove that it was thought to have been constructed on the same basic design as Solomon's temple in Jerusalem.

THE SONGS OF THE SABBATH SACRIFICE

Aware for some time of the existence among the Dead Sea Scrolls of a substantial body of material from a kind of heavenly liturgy, scholars had been impatiently awaiting its publication. They were not disappointed. In 1985 Carol Newsom published a critical edition of what she called *The Songs of the Sabbath Sacrifice*, a correlation of numerous fragments, some large, some small, of manuscripts from Qumran and (a single fragment only) Masada, painstakingly assembled and forming yet another clear proof that merkabah mysticism had been practiced in many Jewish circles in the Second Temple era (the period preceding the destruction of the temple in 70 C.E.).

ABOVE: *The fortress of Masada, just south of the Dead Sea, was once King Herod's summer palace. It is best known as the scene of the Jewish Zealots' last despairing struggle against the besieging Romans, led by the future emperor, Titus. Having held this stronghold for seven years, they refused to surrender, and the siege ended with their joint suicide in 73 C.E. Masada is also where, in 1963-64, archaeological researchers discovered further precious fragments of the Dead Sea Scrolls.*

"The cherubim lie prostrate before him and bless. As they rise a whispered divine voice is heard, and there is a roar of praise. When they raise their wings there is a whispered divine voice. The cherubim bless the image of the chariot-throne above the vault of the cherubim, and they sing the majesty of the luminous firmament beneath his seat of glory. And when the ofanim [wheels] advance the holy angels retire; they emerge among the glorious wheels with the likeness of fire, the spirits of the Holy of Holies. Around them, the likeness of a stream of fire like amber, and a luminous substance with glorious colors, wonderfully intermingled, brightly combined. The spirits of the living gods move constantly with the glory of the wonderful chariots. And there is a whispered voice of blessing in the roar of their motion, and on returning to their paths they praise the Holy One. When they rise, they rise wonderfully, and when they settle, they are prepared. The voice of glad rejoicing becomes silent and there is a whispered blessing of the gods in all the camps of the gods."

FAR RIGHT: *Paul struck blind on the Damascus Road. A 12th-century mosaic in the Palatine Chapel, in the royal palace of the Norman kings of Sicily. This is the first of a cycle of illustrations of St Paul's life set around the chapel's walls.*

BELOW: *Jacopi Tintoretto (1518-94) called this picture* Paradise. *For him, as for many others, the true Paradise was now in heaven.*

The preceding paragraph, excerpted from *The Songs of the Sabbath Sacrifice*, represents the culmination of a tradition of divine worship going back at least as far as the vision of Ezekiel. Here we have an assembly of variously named heavenly beings (gods, angels, spirits, priests, sovereign princes, holy ones) proclaiming the praise of the Lord over a succession of seven sabbaths.

Here we have a mixture of old and new. Old, reaching right back into the remote past of Israel's Canaanite heritage, is the picture of one supreme God, El, enthroned in the center of a court of lesser gods, spirits, or angel-priests, who lift up their voices in a song of praise. (Elsewhere he is called "the God of the gods of the chiefs of the heights, and king of the kings of all the eternal councils.") New are the myriad voices that accompany them. The cherubim had long been personalized as angels, but elsewhere in the document the wheels (*ofanim*) also join in the song; so do the chariots (now in the plural), the various parts of the temple ("its beams, its walls, its shape, the work of its construction"), and even the inner sanctum (*debir*) itself. Read in its entirety, the document presents us with a dazzling display of orchestrated praise resounding in a well-populated heaven.

THE FOUR RABBIS

Although Hebrew, like Greek, did eventually come to borrow from Persian the word "paradise," the relatively rare instances of the term *pardes*, both in the Bible and elsewhere, signify nothing more than "garden" or "orchard." When the rabbis wished to refer to what we call Paradise they spoke of *gan 'eden*, the Garden of Eden. So in the well-known story of the four rabbis who suffered various fates after rashly entering a garden, the term *pardes* was most likely used as a symbolic way of referring to the study (in this case the unsupervised study) of the Bible. But by the time it had been taken over by the Babylonian Talmud (fifth century C.E.) it had come to refer to paradise (in heaven),

and to the dangers of attempting a mystical ascent without taking due precautions. Here is an abbreviated version of the tale:

Four men entered a garden. They were Ben Azzai, Ben Soma, Aher (= A. N. Other) and R. Akiba. R. Akiba said to them, "When you approach the stones of pure marble, do not say, Water, water, for it is written, He who speaks lies will not tarry in my presence." Ben Azzai looked and died. Ben Zoma looked and was struck. Aher cut the plants [!] R. Akiba went up in peace and came down in peace. The Holy One, Blessed be He, said to them, "Leave this elder alone, for he is worthy to avail himself of my glory."

So Ben Azzai died, Ben Zoma went mad, and Aher abandoned his Jewish faith. Only Akiba survived unscathed. These rabbis were pictured, like Enoch, as entering the great hall of the temple. The stones of pure marble which they are forbidden to think of as water must belong to the floor or wall of the heavenly palace, so this story has come to be associated with merkabah mysticism. A passage in the Mishnah remarks upon the particular dangers associated with the study of the chariot throne chapter, the source, as we have seen, of this important mystical tradition. One late rabbinical commentator on this passage, Hananel b. Hushiel, tells

The Apostle Paul

*P*aul, the true founder of the Christian religion, might seem out of place in a chapter on Jewish ideas of Paradise. But from his description of how he was "snatched up" into Paradise, and carried up "as far as the third heaven" it is clear that his experience resembles the one recorded in 2 Enoch, in which Paradise is similarly located below the third heaven. Paul, notoriously coy about his mystical experiences, says nothing about what he saw, but adds that "in order to prevent me from being carried up too far a thorn was given me in the flesh, an angel of Satan to buffet me, to keep me from being carried up too far." This suggests that he shared in the negative experience of certain Jewish mystics, such as the Rabbi Akiba who, in one version of his own ascent to pardes, speaks of "angels of destruction" who attempted to do him violence. Even Paul's conversion on the Damascus Road is likely to have occurred as a consequence of a mystical experience akin to the Jewish merkabah mysticism which he—a highly educated religious Jew—had inherited.

us that "*pardes* was used as a term for the Garden of Eden, which was reserved for the righteous." As time passed the Garden of Eden (the Hebrew phrase was still much more common) was increasingly thought by the rabbis to be located in heaven. Christianity, as we shall see, held on to the notion of an earthly paradise much longer, but there too the idea of a heavenly paradise, which may have been present as early as the New Testament, eventually took over completely.

SHEOL: LIFE AFTER DEATH

The Jewish Sheol is almost the exact equivalent of the Homeric Hades. Both are regions of gloom inhabited by whispering ghosts who lead a shadowy existence in the underworld, the realm of the dead—Sheol is a place in which even God himself is forgotten: "For in death there is no remembrance of thee; in Sheol who will give thee praise?" According to the oldest Jewish tradition this is where all the dead went, both good and bad, as the account of King David's final commission to his son Solomon makes quite clear:

"When David's time to die drew near, he charged Solomon, his son, saying, 'I am about to go the way of all the earth. Be strong and show yourself a man. You know what Joab the son of Jeruiah did to me. Act therefore according to your wisdom and do not let his head go down to Sheol in peace. Hold him not guiltless, for you are a wise man; you will know what you ought to do to him, and bring his head down with blood to Sheol.'"

David has no need to spell out the nature of his journey, nor his goal: the way of all the earth leads in one direction only, that of Sheol. The only difference between David's death and the one he is arranging for Joab to settle their vendetta lies in the manner of their

NOBILIS PATRIARCHARVM CETVS

The Witch of Endor

Toward the end of his reign when everything began to go wrong, Saul became unable to take any decision without some sort of divine guidance. The standard procedures for divine consultation having failed, Saul turned for help to the Witch of Endor, a necromancer. (Necromancy is a method for summoning up spirits from the dead, a practice that Saul himself had earlier outlawed.) At first the witch, who did not recognize him, showed some reluctance: "Surely you know what Saul has done, how he has cut off the necromancers and the wizards from the land. Why then are you laying a snare for my life to bring about my death?" Saul swore that she would come to no harm, and so she proceeded to call up the prophet Samuel, Saul's guide and mentor who had anointed him Israel's first king. On seeing Samuel, "she cried out with a loud voice; and the woman said to Saul, 'Why have you deceived me? You are Saul.' The king said to her, 'Have no fear; what do you see?' And the woman said to Saul, 'I see a god coming up out of the earth.' He said to her, 'What is his appearance?' And she said, 'An old man is coming up; and he is wrapped in a robe.' And Saul knew that it was Samuel, and he bowed with his face to the ground, and did obeisance." Emerging as he does from Sheol, Samuel is still no more than a ghost. He has no place on earth and soon returns to the realm of the dead.

SAUL AND THE WITCH OF ENDOR

departures. His own death, he hopes, will be peaceful; Joab's, if he can manage it, will be bloody. Their destination is the same.

At one point in the Book of Job—which in its form curiously resembles a classical Greek tragedy—the wretched protagonist inveighs against his fate. There is no surer proof of the extent of his misery than his prayer to be hidden away in Sheol. He has no illusions about the finality of death and he complains of it to God in strong, bitter poetry. For Job the best image of human death is not a tree, which ensures its own survival by sprouting new shoots, but stones worn down by continuously dripping water or a mountain collapsing under its own weight. Elsewhere he says that Sheol is his home and darkness his bed; he has the grave for a mother and decay for a sister. No hope here of immortality, and no hint of a future resurrection.

"For there is hope of a tree, if it be cut down, that it will sprout again, and that the tender branch thereof will not cease. Though the root thereof wax old in the earth, and the stock thereof die in the ground, yet through the scent of water it will bud, and bring forth boughs like a plant. But man dieth, and wasteth away: yea, man giveth up the ghost, and where is he? If a man die, shall he live again? And surely the mountain falling cometh to nought, and the rock is removed out of his place. The waters wear the stones: thou washest away the things which grow out of the dust of the earth; and thou destroyest the hope of man. Thou prevailest for ever against him, and he passeth: thou changest his countenance, and sendest him away. His sons come to honor, and he knoweth it not; and they are brought low, but he perceiveth it not of them. But his flesh upon him shall have pain, and his soul within him shall mourn."

THE RESURRECTION OF THE BODY

"For I know that my redeemer liveth, and that he shall stand at the latter day upon the earth. And though worms destroy this body, yet in my flesh shall I see God. Whom I shall see for myself, and mine eyes shall behold, and not another; though my reins be consumed within me."

These lines, which provide the text for one of the most beautiful arias in Handel's *Messiah*, were first spoken by Job. They seem to stand in flat contradiction to his despairing outburst quoted earlier, and might even be taken as evidence of an early belief in the resurrection of the dead. But this would be wrong. Scholars now think that all Job looks for after his death is a brief glimpse from the underworld of the vindication he had sought on earth. Although Job may be feeling more optimistic than he did before, there is no hope here of bodily resurrection. He is simply saying that when life seems a bit easier to bear the prospect of death depresses him less.

In the second century B.C.E., however—long after the composition of Job—there does appear evidence of a belief in the resurrection of the dead. It arrives in the prophecy of Daniel: "And many of those that sleep in the dust of the earth shall awake, some to everlasting life, and some to shame and everlasting contempt."

Daniel evidently thought that the good and the wicked would rise together; but the men and women

ABOVE: The Resurrection of the Dead *by Luca Signorelli (c.1445-1523). This fresco, in the Saint Brixio Chapel, Orvieto Cathedral, portrays the dead rising out of the stony ground, and then strutting around conversing with one another. This picture is balanced by a composition on another wall that shows the damned consigned to hell.*

LEFT: *King Saul asks the Witch of Endor to summon the ghost of Samuel from the dead. From an evangelical 19th-century Bible.*

The Valley of the Bones

*E*zekiel's famous vision of the Valley of the Bones is really no more than a vivid and extended metaphor expressing his passionate belief in the future transformation and rejuvenation of his own people. "Prophesy upon these bones," he is told, "and say unto them, O ye dry bones, hear the word of the LORD. Thus saith the Lord GOD unto these bones: 'Behold, I will cause breath to enter into you, and ye shall live. And I will lay sinews upon you, and will bring up flesh upon you, and cover you with skin, and put breath in you, and ye shall live; and ye shall know that I am the LORD.'" Everything happened as the Lord had promised, and Ezekiel saw the bones assembled into a great army. "Then he said unto me, Son of man, these bones are the whole house of Israel: behold, they say, Our bones are dried, and our hope is lost: we are cut off for our parts. Therefore prophesy and say unto them, Thus saith the Lord GOD; Behold, O my people, I will open your graves, and cause you to come up out of your graves, and bring you into the land of Israel. And ye shall know that I am the LORD, when I have opened your graves, O my people, and brought you up out of your graves; and I shall put my spirit in you, and ye shall live, and I shall place you in your own land: then shall ye know that I the LORD have spoken it, and performed it, saith the LORD."

who accepted the doctrine of the resurrection of the body spoke of it as reserved for the righteous and the wise. It was a sectarian belief, an additional resource for distinguishing the good guys (the members of the sect) from the bad guys (the rest of society) and for retaining a sense of their own superiority to outsiders. In the Book of the Watchers Enoch is told of the arrangements made to separate the souls of the just, awaiting resurrection, from the souls of the wicked. The doctrine was adopted by the Pharisees, who condemned their rivals, the Sadducees, for refusing to accept it. According to the Mishnah, people who deny the resurrection of the dead are themselves doomed not to rise.

There is an episode in the life of Paul, under arrest in Jerusalem, when he is hauled before the chief priests and the Sanhedrin (council). Realizing that he is confronting two mutually hostile groups, he is smart enough to exploit their differences: "Brethren," he says, "I am a Pharisee, a son of Pharisees; with respect to the hope and the resurrection of the dead I am on trial." Whereupon, Luke tells us, "a dissension arose between the Pharisees and the Sadducees; and the assembly was divided. For the Sadducees say that there is no resurrection, nor angel, nor spirit; but the Pharisees acknowledge them all."

Paul's own belief in the resurrection had been given a great boost by his vision, on the road to Damascus, of the crucified and risen Christ. This convinced him that Christ was truly risen from the dead and it was this faith, shared by his converts, that marked out Christianity from Judaism and came to figure prominently in all Christian creeds. "If Christ has not been raised," Paul tells the Corinthians, "then our preaching is in vain and your faith is in vain." And this faith must extend to the general resurrection of the dead: "For if the dead are not raised, then Christ has not been raised. If Christ has not been raised, your faith is futile and you are still in your sins."

THE IMMORTALITY OF THE SOUL

ABOVE: *The weighing of the dead at the last judgment portrayed in a miniature from a 13th-century psalter.*

Belief in the immortality of the soul fits uneasily, if at all, with the doctrine of bodily resurrection. There is no clear evidence for this belief in the Bible itself, although Josephus ascribes it to the sect of the Essenes, widely thought to have included in their numbers the dissident Jews who had taken refuge in the caves of Qumran.

The most prominent Jew to have professed this belief was the philosopher Philo of Alexandria, who frequently argues for it in his abundant writings. He was evidently influenced by Plato, who regarded the soul as the prisoner of the body. Death in this context was thought of as a liberation.

It is another Jewish text, however, composed probably in the first century B.C.E. and emanating, like Philo, from Alexandria, that gives us the clearest evidence of a belief in immortality. The Wisdom of Solomon is included in the Greek Bible, and therefore accepted as inspired by both the Orthodox and the Catholic churches. Its reading of the Genesis story is that God planned from the outset to grant immortality to the human race: "for God created man for incorruption, and made him in the image of his own eternity, but through the devil's envy death entered the world, and those who belong to his party experience it."

"There was one who pleased God and was loved by him, and while living among sinners he was taken up. He was caught up lest evil change his understanding or guile deceive his soul... Being perfected in a short time, he fulfilled long years; for his soul was pleasing to the Lord, therefore he took him quickly from the midst of wickedness. Yet the peoples saw and did not understand, nor take such a thing to heart, that God's grace and mercy are with his elect, and he watches over his holy ones."

Like numerous other Jewish writers this author alludes to the exceptional fate of Enoch, though as usual when speaking of Jewish heroes he does not actually name him. Nor is he concerned to inform his readers of the site of Enoch's current habitation.

A similar belief in the immortality of the soul is often ascribed to early Christian writers, even on occasion to Saint Paul, though it was certainly never part of his faith or of his message. It was eventually absorbed into Christian teaching as a consequence of the influence of the neo-Platonists. In this respect, as in many others, Christianity followed the lead of its parent religion.

PARADISE REGAINED

THE OPEN DOOR

The fourth chapter of the Book of Revelation (revelation is the literal translation of the Greek word apocalypse) starts with a vision of an extraordinary scene in heaven. "I looked," says the seer, John, "and lo, in heaven, an open door!" Suddenly he hears a voice calling to him "like a trumpet," and thereupon sees a throne with a seated figure. "And he who sat there appeared like jasper and carnelian, and round the throne was a rainbow that looked like an emerald." The two stones were among those worn by the King of Tyre on his priestly breastplate, and the appearance of a rainbow marked the peaceful conclusion of Ezekiel's storm vision. Enoch, long before, had also seen an open door after being caught up into the heavens and entering the first of two great houses. In both cases we read of a heavenly temple and the entry into the inner of its two courts. In the Testament of Levi, an apocryphal Christian writing, Levi's vision starts on top of a mountain, perhaps the mountain of paradise: "and I beheld a high mountain, and I was on it. And behold, the heavens were opened, and an angel of the Lord spoke to me: 'Levi, Levi, enter.'" He obeys, and further on another door opens: "And I saw the Most High sitting on a throne."

Levi, like John and Enoch before him, was simply following the lead of the prophet Ezekiel, the first to have had a vision of the All Highest seated on a throne. We are witnessing the culmination of a strong mystical tradition, several centuries old.

Round the central throne John observes 24 other thrones, all occupied by figures he calls elders, dressed in white and wearing golden crowns. Lightning flashes are followed by peals of thunder, and in front of the central throne "there is as it were a sea of glass, like crystal." This recalls Ezekiel's vision, with its firmament of crystal, and Enoch's, where the throne itself is

said to resemble crystal. But the true origin of the sea of glass is the sea above the sky that floats on the firmament separating heaven and earth. Psalm 104 (a creation psalm) says of God that he has "stretched out the heavens like a tent" and "laid the beams of his chambers on the waters."

Next John notices the four living creatures who encircle the throne, "full of eyes in front and behind." They are first cousins to the creatures in Ezekiel's vision, but simplified, in that they now have but one face each—lion, ox, man, and flying eagle—with six wings apiece. "Holy, holy, holy," they sing unceasingly, "is the Lord God Almighty."

THE NEW EDEN

The concluding chapters of the Book of Revelation are like an elaborate tapestry in which most of the various motifs associated with Eden or paradise are ingeniously intertwined. Chapter 21 begins with a vision of a new heaven and a new earth, the descent of the new Jerusalem "prepared as a bride adorned for her husband," and the assuaging of all grief. Jerusalem, surrounded by a great high wall with 12 gates, is described as having a radiance like jasper, "clear as crystal" and being made of pure gold, "clear as glass." Twelve precious stones, including jasper and carnelian, adorn the city wall.

The chapter that follows confirms this hint that we might be close to paradise. The seer is shown "the river of the water of life, bright as crystal, flowing from the throne of God" and "the tree of life with its twelve kinds of fruit, yielding its fruit each month" which appears to cover with its foliage both sides of the river. Twelve kinds of fruit—just as the city has 12 gates, each made of a single pearl and inscribed with the name of one of the 12 tribes of Israel, and the city wall has 12 foundations, each with its own precious stone. Here as in much apocalyptic writing the description leaves the imagination reeling, but we are not meant to try to build up a composite picture with every detail in its proper place: what counts is the collective impact of the intricate design. But there can be no doubt that we are back in Eden, its garden splendidly restored, with the abundant fruit of the tree of life at last available for the picking.

The main biblical source (there are dozens) of John's vision of the New Jerusalem is to be found in the concluding chapters of Ezekiel, one of the longest books in the Bible. At the heart of Ezekiel's earlier vision is the construction of the new temple that will replace the old, harlot-dominated temple that Ezekiel hated and despised. And at the heart of the new temple will be the abiding presence of God: "this is the place of my throne and the place of the soles of my feet, where I will dwell in the midst of the people of Israel for ever." So when John says, "I saw no temple in the city," this comes as a shock. John's New Jerusalem is to be radically different from the old.

ABOVE: The Garden of Eden *by Jan Bruegel, who was evidently more interested in the flora and fauna of paradise than in the human couple, the two tiny figures toward the center of the picture. A copy of this painting by his grandson Jan van Kessel is on the cover of this book.*

RIGHT: This Russian icon (c.1674) by Ignati Panteleev centers upon the prophet Elijah's ascent into heaven in a fiery chariot at the end of his life, as recorded in 2 Kings, 2:11. The surrounding panels depict various episodes of Elijah's eventful career, including the most famous of his miracles, the raising to life of the dead child of the widow of Zarephath described in 1 Kings 17:19.

OPPOSITE: The despairing Elijah had pleaded with God to allow him to die in the desert; but God's answer was to send an angel to bring him food: "and as he lay and slept under a juniper tree, behold, then an angel touched him, and said unto him, Arise and eat." (I Kings 19:5).

*I*n the whole of the Bible only two men—Enoch and Elijah—were believed to have been spared death and instead carried up to heaven. Although the *Mekilta*, a second-century midrash (modified version of a biblical text), firmly denies the story of Elijah's ascent, the Bible is explicit. As Elijah was conversing with his friend and disciple Elisha: "Behold, a chariot of fire and horses of fire separated the two of them. And Elijah went up by a whirlwind into heaven. And Elisha saw it and he cried, 'My father, my father! The chariots of Israel and its horsemen!' And he saw him no more."

Later rabbinical traditions elaborate upon the biblical story. After his ascent, we are told, he was confronted on the threshold of heaven by the menacing figure of the Angel of Death, who refused him entrance, claiming that God had given him jurisdiction over all mankind and that Elijah was no exception. God himself supported Elijah: he had given explicit instructions for him to be admitted directly into heaven, but the Angel of Death insisted. The rest of the human race, he argued, would have a

legitimate complaint if this one man alone were spared the common destiny of doom and death. Seeing that the two opponents were obdurate, God allowed them to fight. Elijah proved the stronger of the two. He was about to annihilate his adversary, when God intervened and held him back. Elijah then ascended triumphantly into heaven, holding his defeated enemy under his feet.

Once in heaven, Elijah passes the time recording the deeds of men and the chronicles of the world. He also acts as a guide to the pious dead, leading them to their appointed place in paradise. Another of his duties is to bring up the souls of sinners from Gehenna (hell) as the Sabbath is approaching and lead them back to their deserved punishment once it is over. When they have atoned for their sins he leads them up to the place of everlasting bliss.

According to biblical tradition Elijah was destined to return to earth as the precursor of the Messiah. The evangelist Matthew identifies him with John the Baptist, who appears in the gospel wearing Elijah's thousand-year-old outfit, "a garment of camel's hair and a leather girdle round his waist."

THE MYSTIC LAMB

All the material used in the previous chapter, The Jewish Paradise, including extracts from the Book of Revelation, is recognizably Jewish. The myths and motifs of the Bible, pushing outside and beyond the confines of the canonical text, provided later generations with a stock of concepts that enabled them to expand and elaborate upon the original stories of Adam and Eve and the King of Tyre.

At the heart of the Book of Revelation stands a Christian symbol that has so far received no mention. This is the symbol of the slaughtered lamb: not the Passover lamb (which is killed for human consumption, not for sacrifice) but an image or type of Christ. The Lamb of Revelation, moreover, once dead but now risen to a new life, is nothing like the cuddly, woolly creature of children's imaginations. This is a powerful, even menacing figure who dominates every scene in which he appears.

On his first appearance, in chapter 5, the Lamb emerges from the crowd of elders to take a scroll from the figure on the throne and to receive the worshipping adulation of "the myriads of myriads and thousands of thousands" of the angels assembled round the throne: "To him who sits on the throne and to the Lamb be blessing and glory and might for ever and ever."

This is unquestionably a Christian scene, but it is nonetheless heavily indebted to a well-known vision of the prophet Daniel, who had observed God (the Ancient of Days) invite a human figure (one like a son of man) to occupy another throne placed beside him. The Christian seer borrows unashamedly from the Jewish apocalypse, which lends his own vision a certain intelligibility.

The Lamb proceeds to open a series of seven seals. The opening of the fourth seal sees the entry of a pale horse, whose rider's name is Death. The opening of the sixth seal is followed by the humble obeisance of "the kings of the earth and the generals and the rich and the strong," who call out to the mountains and rocks where they have taken refuge: "Fall on us and hide us from the face of him who is seated on the throne, and from the wrath of the Lamb."

When Satan is hurled precipitately from heaven it is by the power of the blood of the Lamb, and it is foretold that the Lamb will assist at the unremitting torture ("with fire and sulphur") of anyone who worships the wicked beast. This is the

ABOVE: Jan van Eyck (c.1390-1441).The Adoration of the Lamb from the Altarpiece in St. Bavo Cathedral, Ghent, 1426. The Lamb is shown surrounded by worshipping angels and elders. The fountain in the foreground evidently represents the river of the water of life, bright as crystal, flowing from the throne of God and of the Lamb, words drawn from the opening verse of the final chapter of the Book of Revelation, the culmination and conclusion of the whole Christian Bible.

beast whose number, as the seer mysteriously informs us, "is a human number: its number is six hundred and sixty-six".

Kings who dare to make war on the Lamb will be conquered, "for he is the Lord of lords and the King of kings"; and eventually the Lamb appears in the new city of Jerusalem, where he is seen to have done away with any need to retain the old temple and the worship conducted within it: for now the temple of the city "is the Lord God Almighty and the Lamb." In this wholesale dismissal of the Temple, which stood, along with the Law, as one of the twin pillars of ancient Judaism, the Christian reader will recognize the arrival not only of a new Eden, but of a new religion.

ANGELS
OF ISLAM

Chapter

6

The Quran stresses the importance of Adam and Eve who are created by God as the foreparents of the whole human race. They are tempted by Satan, sin in the garden and subsequently live outside it. Life on earth involves moral choice: following God will lead to paradise but falling for Satan's guiles will lead to the horrors of the fire of hell.

LEFT: The double title page from a 16th-century Persian Quran. Muslims believe that the Quran is the Word of God, revealed to the Prophet Mohammed in early 7th-century Arabia by the Archangel Gabriel.

THE GARDENS OF DELIGHT

In Islam the Quran is the sacred book, the holy word of God, revealed to the Prophet Mohammed by Gabriel, the angel of revelation. The word *quran* means "reading"; the text of the Quran lies at the center of the Islamic faith and the concept of the Gardens of Paradise lies at the heart of the Quran. Nearly every chapter (or *surah*) mentions paradise and it is a crucial theme within the religion of Islam.

The Quran, like the Bible, contains the story of Adam and Eve, although the versions differ in certain key areas. The Quran also contains frequent descriptions of the Gardens of Paradise, as the abode of the righteous in the hereafter.

Both Eden and heaven are described by the Arabic word *al-janna*, which means "the Garden." It is a true paradise. The root of the word *janna* is "veiling" or "covering," which is clearly close to the "enclosure" of the Persian *pairidaeza*. Situated close to the Garden is hell—but the Garden is "veiled" or enclosed: its occupants are under no threat from the evildoers who burn in the fire of hell.

THE STORY OF ADAM AND EVE

In the Quran's interpretation of this story, God creates Adam and Eve out of dust. He creates Adam first, and then Eve, and both are generated from a single soul. God ordains love and mercy between them: He has created them as spouses, so that both may find repose.

God wishes to confer authority on Adam and tells the angels to prostrate themselves before Adam as God's pontifex, the mediator between heaven and earth. God does so because he has endowed Adam with the knowledge of the essences of things and with free will, whereas the angels do not necessarily have these two qualities. All the angels prostrate themselves with the exception of Satan (called Iblis), who refuses to prostrate himself—thus rejecting the order that God is establishing in the universe —and insists that he is better than Adam: "thou createdst me of fire while him thou didst create of mud." God responds by exiling Satan from paradise. The Garden is no place for Satan's contemptuous pride. God declares: "Go forth from hence, degraded, banished. As for such of them as follow thee, surely I will fill hell with all of you."

Although God orders Satan out of the Garden as a punishment, Satan asks to be reprieved until the day of judgment. God is not deceived but grants this reprieve, whereupon the motive for Satan's request becomes clear. Satan vows to waylay God's people; he will spring upon them from the front and the rear, from the right and from the left, and make them ungrateful to God.

God tells Satan that he will have no power over those who believe in him, and that he will throw Satan and his followers into hell on the day of judgment. God tells Adam and Eve that they should live in the Garden and enjoy the good things in it as they wish, but that they should not eat the fruit from "this tree." The Quran does not state which tree this is, although traditional Islamic commentaries agree it to be the Tree of Knowledge of Good and Evil.

Satan dramatically reappears in Eden to lead Adam and Eve astray, tempting Adam and Eve by saying that God has forbidden them to approach the tree only to prevent their becoming angels or immortals. He cunningly seduces them, swearing that he is their

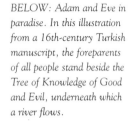

BELOW: Adam and Eve in paradise. In this illustration from a 16th-century Turkish manuscript, the foreparents of all people stand beside the Tree of Knowledge of Good and Evil, underneath which a river flows.

He it is Who created for you all that is in the earth.
Then turned He to the heaven, and fashioned it as
seven heavens. And He is Knower of all things.

And when thy Lord said unto the angels: Lo! I am
about to place a viceroy in the earth, they said:
Wilt Thou place therein one who will do harm therein
and will shed blood, while we, we hymn Thy praise
and sanctify Thee?
He said: surely I know that which ye know not.

And He taught Adam all the names, then showed them
to the angels, saying: Inform Me of the names of these,
if ye are truthful.

They said: Be glorified! We have no knowledge saving
that which Thou hast taught us. Lo! Thou, only Thou,
art the Knower, the Wise.

He said: O Adam! Inform them of their names, and
when he had informed them of their names, He said:
Did I not tell you that I know the secret of the heavens
and the earth? And I know that which ye disclose and
which ye hide.

And when We said unto the angels: Prostrate yourselves before Adam, they fell prostrate, all save Iblis.
He demurred through pride, and so became a disbeliever.

And We said: O Adam! Dwell thou and thy wife in
the Garden, and eat ye freely (of the fruits) thereof
where ye will; but come not nigh this tree lest ye
become wrong-doers.

But Satan caused them to deflect therefrom and
expelled them from the (happy) state in which they
were; and We said: Fall down, one of you a foe unto
the other!

Then Adam received from his Lord words
(of revelation), and He relented toward him.
Lo! He is the Relenting, the Merciful.

We said: Go down, all of you from hence; but verily
there cometh unto you from Me a guidance; and whoso
followeth My guidance, there shall no fear come upon
them neither shall they grieve.

But they who disbelieve, and deny Our revelations,
such are rightful owners of the Fire. They will abide
therein.
THE QURAN, 2, 29-39

RIGHT: The Court of the Canal in the garden of the
Generalife at the Alhambra in Granada, Spain. The gardens
and architecture of the largely 14th-century Alhambra palaces
deliberately evoke Quranic images of paradise with the sights
and sounds of running water and access to cooling shade.

ABOVE: Adam and Eve holding hands in the Garden, from an early 17th-century Turkish miniature. The flames around their heads are the equivalent of haloes.

shall be the heirs of hell. God urges the children of Adam (by implication, all people) not to let Satan seduce them. "Lo! He seeth you, he and his tribe, from whence ye see him not." One must therefore be vigilant against evil.

THE MORAL OF THE STORY

Although the Quran's account of Adam and Eve has close links to the Book of Genesis, it is told very differently. The Bible tells its history chronologically, from the beginning to the end of time, and so the story of Adam and Eve occurs early in Genesis, the first book of the Bible. The account of Eden is not at the start of the Quran and while its readers are welcome to believe that the passages about Adam and Eve are historically true, historical truth is not the point of their story.

Adam and Eve are central characters in the Eden story, but they are there to serve a purpose within broader teachings about the primordial origin of man, for Adam is a prophet in Islam and the Adamic state is the goal of every Muslim. Often, they are not mentioned by name but are alluded to with the considerable poetic subtlety that Arabic allows, to make a point.

Crucial to the Quran's account is the idea that Adam and Eve are a united pair. Although Adam may (just) have been created before Eve, both are created from a single soul. In Genesis, God creates Adam first and then Eve from Adam, which seems to give the biblical Adam superior status over Eve. In the Quran, there is no Adam's rib: Adam and Eve are a team, a married couple and marriage is an excellent thing. It is the way of the Prophet. It also instils "repose," a state of peace and stillness that is an essential part of paradise. Without this marriage, paradise would have been a lonely place. Adam and Eve, then, may have been the first people—the foreparents of all people—but their importance also lies in being the first married couple.

LEAVING THE GARDEN

Because Adam and Eve eat the fruit, they leave the Garden. They eat the fruit together, as a pair (whereas in Genesis Eve ate first), and since they both disobeyed God, one is not to be blamed more than the other. Indeed, the very word "blame" is far less applicable to this account than it is in Genesis, where Adam and Eve each try to pass on the blame. In the Quran's account they are united and, like all good couples, they share the responsibility of falling for Satan's guile; God's warning had been made to them both. They own up to their wrongdoing and, out of repentance, they ask for forgiveness. God is merciful and

sincere adviser. They eat the fruit of the tree. When they eat the fruit, their shame becomes visible to them: they become aware of their nakedness and they begin to clothe themselves with some of the leaves of the Garden, a sign of the loss of primordial innocence. They immediately ask for forgiveness: "Our Lord! We have wronged ourselves. If thou forgive us not and have not mercy on us, surely we are of the lost." God responds by sending them out of the Garden: "There will be for you on earth a habitation and provision for a while … there shall ye live and there shall ye die, and thence shall ye be brought forth." God makes it clear that this is not a wholly negative fate. Whoever follows God's revelation shall have nothing to fear or to grieve over. Those who deny and reject God's revelation, on the other hand,

ABOVE: *The Prophet Ali Husein and his brother Hasan in Paradise, from the Khavarannameh, 1686. Shi'ah Muslims believe Ali Husein to be the second son of Fatimah, the daughter of Mohammed.*

God of the Bible expelled Adam and Eve, putting them in a state of exile from him that for Christians was only resolved by the redemptive cross, the God of the Quran remains close to his creation, for Adam and Eve repented. God offers a return to paradise as a possibility for the future. This is surely a blessing in disguise. Similarly, part of Eve's punishment in Genesis is woman's pain in childbirth, part of Adam's is that he must labor. These punishments are entirely absent here, but that does not mean they are contradicted.

As a consequence of Adam and Eve's actions—and, crucially, their repentance—God gives them some advice: if they remain true to him and follow his guidance they shall have nothing to fear or grieve over. God is telling them that life on earth is not a loss, that death is not the end. It is also an opportunity for them to learn that obedience is no easy task, that the exercising of free will has consequences.

"O Children of Adam! Let not Satan seduce you!" is a central moral message given by God to mankind as a consequence of Eden. Satan is still out there and can see you even when you can't see him. Following God will lead to paradise; succumbing to Satan will lead to the fire of hell. Paradise and hell: the Quran consistently mentions these two alternative destinies alongside each other. Part of the reason for the believers' wish to enter paradise is an awareness of how its wonders differ from the horrors of the fire: to appreciate the true nature of paradise, one must also be aware of the horrors of hell.

THE NATURE OF GOD'S CREATION

In the Quran, God creates Adam from dust. He returns all people to dust; then, from dust, he resurrects them to paradise or to hell. Dust symbolizes the primordial substance—God makes man out of earth but also, in a sense, out of nothing. God is the creator of all things; He has created being from non-being. He says "Be!" and it is. Everything that exists does so through his power and he provides all that is necessary for the spiritual and physical sustenance of the beings that he has created. God favors mankind. Although humans are a small part of his creation, and all aspects of creation show God's glory, all the visible objects of creation—the heavens, the earth, plants, animals, the seas—are useful to man. The Quran constantly emphasizes this in order to show the greatness of God and the favors that mankind enjoys. The earth is a home; the stars act as a guide or "compass"; plants and animals provide food.

forgives them. He takes them from the Garden but this is not a permanent exile—for provided that Adam and Eve (and by implication all people) follow the guidance that God provides, they will eventually return to the Garden.

Leaving the Garden does not, therefore, mean a drastic separation between man and God. Again, a comparison with Genesis is helpful here: whereas the

Angels are invisible to men but they are also an important part of God's creation, natural occupants of paradise. They are God's trusted servants and are

When the event befalleth—
There is no denying that it will befall—
Abasing (some), exalting (others);
When the earth is shaken with a shock
And the hills are ground to powder
So that they become a scattered dust,
And ye will be three kinds:
(First) those on the right hand; what of those
on the right hand?
And (then) those on the left hand; what of those
on the left hand?
And the foremost in the race, the foremost in the race:
Those are they who will be brought nigh
In gardens of delight;
A multitude of those of old
And a few of those of later time.
On lined couches,
Reclining therein face to face.
There wait on them immortal youths
With bowls and ewers and a cup from a pure spring
Wherefrom they get no aching of the head nor any
madness,
And fruit they prefer
And flesh of fowls that they desire.
And (there are) fair ones with wide, lovely eyes,
Like unto hidden pearls,
Reward for what they used to do.
There hear they no vain speaking nor recrimination
(Naught) but the saying: Peace, (and again) Peace.
THE QURAN, 56, 1-26

Allah promiseth to the believers, men and women,
Gardens underneath which rivers flow, wherein they
abide—blessed dwellings in Gardens of Eden. And—
greater (far)!—acceptance from Allah. That is the
supreme triumph.

O Prophet! Strive against the disbelievers and the
hypocrites! Be harsh with them. Their ultimate abode
is hell, a hapless journey's end
THE QURAN, 9, 72–73

RIGHT: A 17th-century Iranian ink-and-watercolor drawing of
a chastely dressed woman standing in a garden, surrounded by
plants and trees. The fine beauty of the idealized woman suggests
that she is a houri standing in paradise.

incapable of sin. They watch over men and protect them, recording their rights and wrongs in anticipation of the day of judgment. Nevertheless, they must bow down to Adam, for God has taught Adam the nature of things. In addition, Adam has free will but angels do not.

THE GARDEN OF HEAVEN IN THE QURAN

God is just. He makes various promises about the afterlife and he will keep those promises. The afterlife consists of two alternative destinies: heaven and hell. Heaven is pure, perfect and eternal, an everlasting home for believers; it is a garden. Hell is the home of the evildoers, the place of torment where the doomed burn in a bottomless pit.

The Quran states that: "The dwellers of the Garden cry unto the dwellers of the Fire: 'We have found that which our Lord promised us (to be) the truth. Have ye (too) found that which your Lord promised the truth?' They say: 'yea, verily!'" Those that fall into the fire will see that given their actions in their worldly life this is what they deserve. This verse may seem a strange way to introduce a discussion about the future garden of bliss but it illustrates how the Quran constantly mentions the Garden and the fire together: it is easier to realize just how wonderful that paradise is while remembering those burning in the fire. Paradise and hell are entirely separate; paradise is enclosed and protected from the evildoers, guarded by gates which swing open to welcome them into the Gardens of Delight.

THE GARDENS OF DELIGHT

Paradise is an eternal place of bliss, laughter, joy, comfort, and ease, a garden in which there is no idle talk or cause of sin, only the saying "Peace, Peace!" One of the most striking features of paradise is that it is spectacularly comfortable. Dressed in silk, the elect will recline upon couches; they will never be too hot or too cold. As they recline, silver goblets will be brought around for them to enjoy. They will be waited on by immortal youths, and God "will slake their thirst with a pure drink."

For people who lived in an arid environment, the idea of plentiful and pure drink must have been even more attractive than the prospect of being able to enjoy it in goblets and on couches. The Quran makes it clear that the occupants of paradise will enjoy fine wine which will not cause drunkenness, a hangover, or quarreling. There is no Quranic account of anyone actually drinking wine in paradise, but clearly there is no sin attached to the idea.

It is not just the wine that is fine. Elsewhere we are told that the drinking vessels are priceless, that the reclining couches are inlaid with precious stones and gold. The elect enjoy themselves in beautiful robes, wearing wonderful perfumes and expensive jewelry. The servants offer around meat and fruits, as well as wine. These descriptions serve to emphasize a simple and important point: paradise will fulfill one's every wish and satisfy every desire. This said, all desires in paradise are essentially spiritual and conform with the nature of the sanctified spirits who dwell in it.

The harsh realities of desert living are no doubt one of the reasons why the Quran is full of images of shade and of water running in rivers, streams, and scented fountains. The Quran frequently calls paradise the garden "underneath which rivers flow." There are rivers of water, milk, wine, and clarified honey. Trees, rich with fruit, provide pleasant shade. The water and shade both symbolize God's mercy in a garden of immortality, eternity, refuge, and bliss.

In the Garden, there will be chaste maidens with restraining glances. These are the houris, the virgins of paradise. The word *houri* comes from the Arabic *hur*, which means astonishment. The Quran promises righteous men a reward for their good actions on the earth: in the Garden they will enjoy lovely maidens as beautiful as pearls, as rubies, as coral. The houris have black eyes and pale skin and live in enclosed pavilions. They are amorous and of a similar age to the men who will enjoy them. They are modest and demure. Elsewhere, we learn that the houris are "purified." By tradition it is not only the houris who are pure—in the Garden, there is no impurity or pollution of any kind.

Throughout history, the account of the houris in the Quran has captured the imagination of believers and non-believers alike. For this reason the houris have often been given a significance they do not really have; they are an interesting aspect of paradise but they should not be regarded as its most essential feature.

Christian critics have often used the houris as an excuse for claiming that all is not well in the Islamic afterlife, criticizing the implication that it includes sex. Yet the Muslim is free to accept that Adam and Eve, in their first paradise, enjoyed sexual relations as the first married couple. The Quran and traditions do refer to the houris as "wives" and the Quran repeatedly makes it clear that all pleasures in paradise have a spiritual dimension. There is no explicit mention of sexual relations in the Garden, and finally sexual union is best understood as an existential symbol in this life for the union between the Lover and the Beloved, or Man and God.

Buraq

Buraq is a magical beast on which Mohammed rides to heaven. The Arabic *buraq* closely relates to the word for "lightning," but some interpreters have insisted that because Buraq is a unique beast, one should not look elsewhere for the origins of its name. In one stride, the creature can cover a distance as far as it can see (this is also a symbolic statement about wisdom: Buraq looks ahead a long way and instantly reaches the destination, the conclusion). One report gives Buraq two wings; other descriptions make him a mixture of horse, ass, and mule; but "a cheek like a man, a mane like a horse, legs like a camel, hooves and tail like an ox, and a chest like a ruby" is more elaborate still. He also is said to have eyes that are brighter than the stars, great intelligence, and the power of human speech. In the story of Mohammed's ascent to heaven, Buraq is brought saddled to Mohammed, with Gabriel holding the stirrup and the Angel Michael holding the reins. Buraq shies away. Gabriel tells the beast that Mohammed is more honored by God than anyone else who has ridden on the animal. Buraq sinks to the ground, ready for Mohammed to ride. In one tradition Buraq says: "is this the mediator who is to teach the new religion of which the fundamental doctrine shall be 'there is no god but God'?" He is. Gabriel replies: "This is Mohammed, prince and seal of the prophets; at his right hand is Paradise, and on his left Hell Fire."

The detailed descriptions of heaven and the afterlife offered in the Quran pale before the remarkable wonders of paradise itself. The descriptions of paradise are symbolic and give the believer an idea of what to hope for. Paradise is beyond the understanding of ordinary mortals—its true wonders will only be shown to the elect. This paradise must be experienced to be understood, and can only be experienced by the resurrected. Full knowledge has not yet been disclosed.

Yet the Quran also describes paradise in the present tense, as though the reader is already in paradise and even now enjoying the wonders of the Garden. The use of the present tense adds intimacy to the account, making the Garden seem close, and reminding believers that paradise is an important reality toward which their spiritual attention should be directed.

RIGHT: A detail of the Archangel Gabriel from an ancient manuscript. Angels were a popular subject in Islamic art, the wings identifying them as the heavenly beings who serve God. Gabriel is often depicted blowing the trumpet of judgment day but is depicted here inspiring Mohammed.

MOHAMMED'S NIGHT JOURNEY: THE ASCENT TO HEAVEN

The important story of Mohammed's ascent to heaven, the Mi'raj, in which the Prophet travels to heaven on the divine horse Buraq, forms part of the Hadith, the sayings of the Prophet Mohammed recorded by his companions. The original account is brief, although tradition supplies many details. Aspects of other stories—and even other stories complete in themselves—were attached to the account of

LEFT: A 16th-century Turkish manuscript shows the magical beast Buraq flying through the firmament, surrounded by angels.

RIGHT: Mohammed on Buraq and surrounded by angels, from a 16th-century Iranian manuscript. Because of the Prophet's injunction against the making of potentially idolatrous images, Mohammed's face is veiled as a mark of respect.

Mohammed's ascension, so we begin not with the journey itself but with the washing of Mohammed's heart, a story which may have its roots in pre-Islamic myths about the weighing of souls.

THE PURIFICATION OF THE HEART

One night Mohammed is in Mecca and the Angel Gabriel descends. Gabriel opens Mohammed's chest and removes his heart. He washes it in a golden basin full of the water of faith, and then restores it to its proper place. (In one version, Gabriel cleanses the heart of blood clots and throws them away.) Mohammed is thus purified: doubt, idolatry, paganism, and error are removed from him. He is filled with belief and wisdom and ready for his journey. The story has at its source chapter 94 of the Quran, which states: "have we not enlarged thy breast," referring to the opening of the heart to the vision of God.

Gabriel has brought with him the magical beast Buraq, upon which the prophets used to ride in ages gone by. Mohammed rides Buraq and dismounts in Jerusalem, where Buraq is tethered to an iron ring put near the temple by Solomon. Mohammed enters the temple and joins Abraham, Moses, and Jesus in prayer, before resuming the next stage of his miraculous journey to heaven.

THE JOURNEY TO HEAVEN

Some Hadith reject the idea that Buraq was involved in the journey to heaven. Rather than having, as is more common, Mohammed sitting on Buraq and being guided by Gabriel whose hand he is holding, they see the Mi'raj as a ladder or stairway. In this report, steps of silver and gold are placed before Gabriel and Mohammed until they reach heaven. One account says of this sight: "I heard the Prophet say: 'the Mi'raj was brought to me. I had never seen anything more beautiful. This is what the deceased looks at when he dies.'" Adorned with pearls, with angels on the right and on the left, the ladder was brought down from heaven for Mohammed's use.

Do you want to enter paradise?
To walk the path of truth
you need the grace of God.
We all face death in the end.
But on the way, be careful
never to hurt a human heart!
MEVLANA JALALUDDIN RUMI

ABOVE: A 16th-century Iranian miniature of Izrail, the Angel of Death. Izrail carries the soul away from the body at the hour of death.

THE SEVEN HEAVENS

They ascend beyond the realm of earthly space and time. The Archangel Gabriel, who reveals himself as a heavenly being, guides Mohammed toward the Absolute. According to the Quran, God created seven heavens. The seven heavens are the degrees of Being which separate creation from the Absolute. Gabriel takes Mohammed to each of the heavens in turn and Mohammed meets the Prophets with whom he prayed in Jerusalem. Adam is in the first and Abraham is in the seventh, with Jesus, John, Aaron, Moses, and Enoch in each of the others. These heavens are represented by the seven celestial bodies: the sun, the moon, and the five visible planets. As Mohammed passes through the gates of each heaven, the messenger in that heaven greets him. There are many accounts of the seven heavens. In one version, the heavens are the named as the abodes of Majesty, Peace, Eden, Retreat, Immortality, the Firdaws (paradise), and Delight. A different rendition places Eden at the summit of a hierarchy of heavens: first Mohammed visits the abode of the Garden of Majesty, which is made of white pearl, then the abode of Peace (red sapphire). Third, he enters the Garden of Refuge (chrysolite), fourth, the Garden of Eternity (yellow coral). The white silver Garden of Bliss is fifth, the red gold Garden of Firdaws is sixth. The seventh garden is Eden and is made of white pearl; it is higher than all other gardens.

THE BOUNDARY OF HEAVEN

At the summit of his ascent, Mohammed reaches a lote tree (jujube tree, which is thorny and has edible fruit). This is the Lote Tree of the Uppermost Limit (or Far Boundary) referred to in the Quran. The Lote Tree marks the end of knowledge, the limit of Being, before the Absolute. Beyond it is the highest mystery of the Divine Essence. According to one tradition the tree is veiled in indescribable colors. In another, it has three attributes: shade, delicious fruit, and a delightful scent; these three features symbolize action, intent, and speech. The tree is sometimes depicted as being so bright that it dazzles the eye, and having its roots growing above and its branches growing down, so that its shade falls on heaven and earth, with fruit like pitchers and leaves like the ears of elephants.

Gabriel now appears in all his splendor and a Divine Light descends, covering the tree and all around it. Mohammed does not lower his eyes, and receives the command from God that men should pray 50 times each day. When Mohammed descends, Moses advises Mohammed that people are weak and that the Prophet should return to God and ask that this number be lowered; it is finally reduced to five.

Gabriel accompanies Mohammed back to Jerusalem and then to Mecca, riding on Buraq. Mohammed returns to find that his bedclothes are still warm: the journey to heaven and back has all taken place in less than a night.

Izrail: the Angel of Death

The Angel of Death is sometimes placed in one of the seven heavens, but in other accounts Mohammed sees him as he rides on his divine horse from one heaven to another. Izrail is so huge it would take 70,000 days to travel from one eye to the other. Other Hadith add further details to Izrail (though not always in the Mi'raj): he is as tall as the distance between earth and heaven, his wing span is huge (so impressive that when he first flew, the other angels fainted at the sight). His wings embrace the faithful, but crush the wicked. God, however, is not intimidated: He created, and is greater than, Izrail.

In medieval paintings, Izrail is sometimes depicted as standing with a foot resting on the bridge that links heaven and hell, over which those who are to be judged must pass. Often, however, Izrail is understood to be accompanied by two sets of angels. The group that stand at his right glow with radiance and have a gentle scent of perfume; they take care of the souls of the chosen. On Izrail's left, angels with black faces and red glowing eyes, who have a noxious odor and voices of thunder, will violently snatch the breath of the wicked and lead them to the fire.

In heaven, there is a book that records all human life: new entries have just been born, entries being erased are the recently deceased. In some versions, this is a book of judgment. In other accounts there is a building which contains objects that will be used to weigh the value of souls.

TOWARD AN UNDERSTANDING

The story of the Mi'raj is closely linked to the themes of paradise, afterlife, and judgment, but it is probably the idea of ascension that has provoked most debate amongst Muslim theologians. Some would prefer to regard Mohammed's journey as a vision or dream, in which heaven and its features are symbols of religious truth. Many regard the Mi'raj as being a journey of the soul: physically, Mohammed sleeps while his purified soul undertakes the journey to the heavens. Many regard the Mi'raj as being a literal journey, involving both body and soul.

Within the story, Mohammed is purified and initiated into a close relationship with God. Sufi mystics have understood the journey as showing how an individual may progress from the narrow confines of his sensual human existence, toward the mystic and divine. At the Lote Tree, the boundary, imagination is set free as one breaks through to an unseen world, watched by Gabriel, the angel of inspiration.

The story of the Mi'raj has reached far beyond the Muslim world and been an important inspiration in the Western arts. It is entirely possible that without the Mi'raj, Dante's *Divine Comedy* would have been very different: Dante wrote his great poem at a time when Latin translations of the Arabic Mi'raj were already available. In structure, his poem can partially be seen as an adaptation of Mohammed's journey: the hero ascending through the circles of heaven toward the throne of God.

May these vows and this marriage be blessed
May it be sweet milk
This marriage, like wine and halva
May this marriage offer fruit and shade
Like the date palm
May this marriage be full of laughter
Our every day a day in Paradise
May this marriage be a sign of compassion
A seal of happiness, here and hereafter
May this marriage have a fair face and a good name
An omen as welcome as the moon in a clear blue sky
I am out of words to describe how spirit mingles
in this marriage.
MEVLANA JALALUDDIN RUMI

BELOW: The Dome of the Rock in Jerusalem, completed in 691 C.E. The mosque became associated with the Mi'raj, believed to be the last point of contact Mohammed had with the earth on the ascent to heaven. In one tradition, the Dome of the Rock marks the spot where Buraq's hoof touched the earth during the journey. The walls of the octagon are decorated with motifs of celestial plants to reflect paradise. The dome may symbolize the dome of heaven.

THE ISLAMIC GARDEN

"You who brought to earth this image of paradise: may the Peace of God stay with you eternally." This medieval inscription on the Fountain of the Lions in the Spanish Alhambra affirms the importance of paradise in the design of courtyards and gardens within Islam. The Islamic garden is a place of retreat and a deliberate enclosure, with walls sheltering its occupants from the unwanted gaze of those outside, the noise of the street, and the unwanted guest. It is also a place of repose and tranquillity: trees and architectural features protect from the harsh daytime sun, the cool of the shade is complemented by the sight and sound of running water, the courtyard and the irrigated plants and trees co-exist in carefully designed unity.

In Islam, paradise is a garden of future bliss promised as a reward to the faithful. The terrestrial Islamic garden deliberately anticipates the heavenly Garden and reflects the beauty of the Garden that has been promised. The visitor to the garden symbolically enters paradise, although the paradise that is to come will far exceed the qualities of human re-creations of it. The garden is thus an important inspiration to theologians, artists, mystics, and poets and should itself be regarded as an art form which creatively adapts the environment: in overwhelmingly arid conditions, the garden is cool and lush, providing color where previously there had been nothing but monotonous dust and harsh surroundings.

Long pre-dating the Islamic era, the Persians enjoyed a secular tradition of a royal pleasure garden or *pairidaeza*, the earliest known dating from the sixth century B.C.E., surrounding the palace of Pasargadae and built by Cyrus the Great. The ruins of that garden (near Isfahan in Iran) include two pavilions, a stone watercourse and pools, as well as a long shaded colonnade. The Persians also believed that the world was symmetrically divided into four zones by two axes forming a cross. Ancient Persian ceramics depict a water pool at the centre of the axes, the point of intersection.

Islam inherited these Persian garden traditions and in using them, its designers emphasized the features of paradise promised in the Quran: pavilions, running water, and shade. Structured geometrically, the gardens are formally planned. A fine example is found in the fourteenth-century Court of the Canal in the gardens of the Generalife at the Alhambra in Granada, Spain (illustrated on page 91). The garden is rectangular, and over fifty metres long. As is typical of Islamic garden design, it is divided into four quarters with a pool at the center, and is enclosed by pavilions. Water is a key feature: the small pool at the center of the garden may symbolize the fountains of paradise and the water of life. Fountains run with water on each side of the waterway and add a quality of meditative calm; the waterway which divides the garden may represent the rivers of paradise mentioned in the Quran. To those attending the nearby mosque, the sights and sounds of gently running water would have been a striking reminder of the pleasures, peace, and serenity promised to the righteous in heaven.

BELOW: Humay and Humayun in the Garden: a 14th-century depiction of a royal couple, from Baghdad. Courtly love and the earthly garden here evoke the beauty and ease of paradise: the lovers sit in a garden filled with flowering plants, enjoying the attention of their attendants, food, and drink.

OPPOSITE: The formal architecture of the Alhambra is an important component of the terrestrial paradise of the garden. Finely carved patios, arches, porches, and halls often overlook the central pools and gardens and provide tranquil and shaded vantage points.

ABOVE
& BELOW

Chapter

7

Paul blamed Adam for introducing death into the world, and much later the doctrine of original sin helped to ensure for the story of Adam and Eve a prominent position in all the medieval media (not newspapers, but Books of Hours; not television, but cathedral windows). Many early Christians were interested in the geographical location of paradise, which figures on all medieval maps of the world. Symbolically too paradise had a role to play in Christian teaching. The tree of life was associated with the cross; whilst the monastic cloister and even the church itself came to be represented by the hortus conclusus, *the enclosed garden, itself thought of as a mini-paradise.*

LEFT: *The cloister of Moyne Abbey in County Mayo, Ireland.*

THE EARLY CHURCH

THE NEW TESTAMENT IN THE OLD

Saint Paul calls Christ a second Adam. What does he mean? When we speak of someone as a second Napoleon, a second Hitler, a second Churchill, we mean that the essential qualities of the first bearer of the name belong equally to the second. But Paul clearly does not want to imply that Christ was in the least like Adam. He saw Adam ("the Man") as someone who wrought ruin upon mankind; Christ, on the contrary, was seen as bringing untold benefits.

This is an early example of what theologians call typology, which is a way of lending a Christian significance to the characters and events of the Old Testament. The "type" (derived from the Greek word typos) can be a person, an event, or a physical object, and it is taken to prefigure some event or person of greater importance. The gospels employ the same device. Jesus is seen as a second Moses because he introduces a new kind of law, and as a second David because he is thought of as a future king, though one whose rule will differ radically from anything that has gone before.

In Christian iconography some Old Testament scenes figure far more frequently than others because they lend themselves more readily to typological interpretation. The Garden of Eden story is one of these scenes.

CHRIST IN THE NEW TESTAMENT

The passion of Jesus and his death upon the cross is by far the longest episode in all four gospels, though treated differently by each. While all four agree that Jesus did not die alone, but was crucified with a robber on either side, Luke alone includes the story of the good thief: he describes how one of the two thieves rebuked the other for joining in the mockery of the bystanders, recognizing that Jesus, alone of the three, had done nothing to deserve punishment. "And he said, 'Jesus, remember me when you come into your kingdom.' And he said to him, 'Truly, I say to you, today you will be with me in Paradise'" (Luke 23:43).

The gospel offers not a word of explanation as to what or where this "paradise" might be, but according to one other New Testament writing—the so-called First Letter of Peter—Jesus still had one final task to fulfill. The passage in question, which records how after his death Jesus "went and preached to the spirits in prison," is crucial for any understanding of what

ABOVE: *Adam, painted in 1528 by Lucas Cranach the elder (1472-1553).*

came to be called "the harrowing of hell." The idea was that a number of biblical figures like Adam and Moses, who obviously could not have known Jesus in the flesh, somehow anticipated his coming and were eager to welcome him. Since there was no question of paradise being available until Jesus had come and opened its gates, these characters, it was believed, had to remain in hell ("prison") until he came to rescue them. The harrowing of hell, an immensely popular theme in Christian imagery and story, portrays Jesus scouring hell in a search for all the good souls, from Adam onward, who had been patiently awaiting his arrival.

It was easy for early Christian writers to form a link between the story in Luke of Jesus' dying words to the good thief and the legend derived from 1 Peter of the harrowing of hell. Many of them were convinced that the paradise in question was none other than the Garden of Eden. Athanasius, bishop of Alexandria in the latter half of the fourth century, goes further and in his *Expositio Fidei* (Exposition of the Faith) actually identifies the thief with Adam: "Jesus has reopened for us the gate of the paradise from which Adam was expelled and has now returned, in the person of the good thief, just as Jesus promised: 'Truly, I say to you, today you will be with me in Paradise.'" Others were less bold, but agreed that the Garden of Eden had indeed been reopened. John Damascene, an eighth-century writer, sums up the views of many of his predecessors in his third book of homilies (Homilia) by enlarging upon Jesus' dying words: "I am he who expelled Adam and Eve from Eden. I will bring you there myself, being the very one who shut the gates of paradise and protected its entrance with a sword of fire."

THE CLASSICAL TRADITION

Unlike Judaism, which resisted the intrusion of most alien influences, Christianity positively welcomed them. The bishops and other clerics who led the church, though no less antagonistic than Jewish rabbis toward the excesses of paganism, shared none of their inhibitions when it came to assimilating for their own purposes the classics of Greek and Roman literature.

The Christian image of paradise had three traditions to draw upon, sometimes distinct, sometimes combined. First there was the Golden Age, which made its first appearance in Hesiod's *Works and Days*, and its most brilliant in Ovid's *Metamorphoses*. Hesiod, introducing a second tradition, placed his bygone heroes in the Isles of the Blessed. The third tradition is that of Elysium (or the Elysian Fields), which the sea

Dives and Lazarus

There was a rich man, who was clothed in purple and fine linen, and fared sumptuously every day; and there was a beggar called Lazarus, who lay at his gate, full of sores, and wanting to feed on the crumbs which fell from the rich man's table. The dogs came and licked his sores. The beggar died, and was carried up by angels into Abraham's bosom: the rich man also died, and went to hell. There, in agony, he raised his eyes and saw Abraham with Lazarus in his bosom. "Father Abraham," he cried, "have mercy on me, and send Lazarus to dip the tip of his finger in water, and cool my tongue; for I am tormented in this flame." But Abraham said, "Son, remember that you were fortunate in your lifetime, and Lazarus unfortunate: but now he is comforted, and you are in agony. Between you and us is fixed a great gulf, which cannot be crossed from either side."

Part of the meaning of this story, which exhibits in exemplary fashion both the best and the worst of the Christian tradition, is that the fate of both men is determined. The rich man's appeal is disallowed: he will suffer in hell forever. Since most well-off people nowadays behave much as he did, we may think his punishment excessively severe—Abraham's vindictiveness and his evident satisfaction in the rich man's misery are hard to swallow. Yet the imaginative sympathy for the plight of the needy, so clearly shown in the story, is equally striking.

ABOVE: *The crucifixicion scene painted by Italian artist Antonello da Messina (1430-1479) c.1460s.*

god Proteus enthusiastically praises to Menelaus in the fourth book of Homer's *Odyssey*: "the gods will lead thee to the dwelling at the end of the earth of the fair-haired Rhadamanthys." To Homer's description of Elysium, Pindar added golden flowers and magnificently branched trees, thereby giving it a closer resemblance to the Garden of Eden; he also gave Elysium a geographical location in the Fortunate Isles.

In the seventh book of *The Odyssey*, there is a variant on the theme of the Fortunate Isles in a description of the garden of Alcinous. This garden is actually an orchard, containing all sorts of fruit-bearing trees. There are pears, pomegranates, golden apples, olives and figs. And of course there are also vines. One Christian writer upon whom this scene left a deep impression was the second-century apologist Justin. In describing an orchard full of beautiful trees and fruits, he argued, Homer was evidently imitating what Moses had said about paradise.

A fourth-century work from Cappadocia, in Asia Minor, illustrates how readily classical traditions can be adapted to a Christian purpose. This work refers to the earthly paradise as an ideal site, safe, handsome, endowed with all the riches of creation, that domi-nated the rest of the world, its air wonderfully limpid, its climate gentle and agreeable. No storms, no hail, no winter ice, no drought nor burning summer heat. In this land of milk and honey the supply of delicious ripe fruit never failed, the meadows were covered throughout the year with a carpet of flowers, and the roses had no thorns. A blessed place, then, free from grief and care; whereas now, the writer concludes, "every time I see a flower I am immediately reminded of my own sins and of the thorns and tribulations by which they have been punished"—the blissful description of pagan innocence has suddenly been overwhelmed by a flood of Christian guilt.

THE MAPPING OF A MYTH

Once the Garden of Eden story has been accepted as a myth, the main problem is how to account for the seemingly precise explanation of the location of the garden. To understand the earnest endeavors of early theologians and geographers to discover the location of paradise, we need to blanket out our modern awareness that they had as much chance of successfully mapping this myth as of capturing a bubble in a box.

A river flowed out of Eden to water the garden, and there it divided and became four rivers. The name of the first is Pishon; it is the one which flows around the whole land of Havilah, where there is gold; and the gold of that land is good; bdellium and onyx stone are there. The name of the second river is Gihon; it is the one, which flows around the whole land of Cush. And the name of the third river is Tigris, which flows east of Assyria. And the fourth river is the Euphrates. GENESIS 2:10-14

EDEN ON EARTH

The Hebrew term *miqqedem*, usually translated as "in the East," is ambiguous—it can also mean "in the

BELOW: Saint Sever's 11th-century map of the world. Adam and Eve, with the snake for good measure, are at the top of the map, which like most medieval maps is oriented with the east positioned where modern cartographers place the north. The Fortunate Isles can be seen below, in the far south-west.

beginning," but the general consensus is now that the former interpretation is correct. Two of the rivers mentioned, the Tigris and the Euphrates, were well known. Rising in the Taurus mountains in eastern Turkey, they flowed the whole length of Mesopotamia (Iraq), branching out briefly into lots of narrow rivulets in the salt marshes of the south before they eventually emptied their waters into the Persian Gulf. (A modern atlas will show them joining together before this, but the confluence may have resulted from the accumulation of silt or alluvium and the consequent displacement of the coastline further south.)

The other two rivers, the Pishon and the Gihon, were harder to identify, leaving interpreters free to speculate. Many early Greek Fathers, taking East to mean the Far East, agreed that they were the Indus and the Ganges. But the Gihon flowed round Cush, which usually meant Ethiopia. The prophet Jeremiah, possibly for this reason, took the name Gihon to refer to the Nile; so did many commentators (including Josephus, who nevertheless continued to think of the Pishon as the Ganges) and this was the view that came to be most widely accepted. All these suggestions might seem to rule out any chance of finding a precise

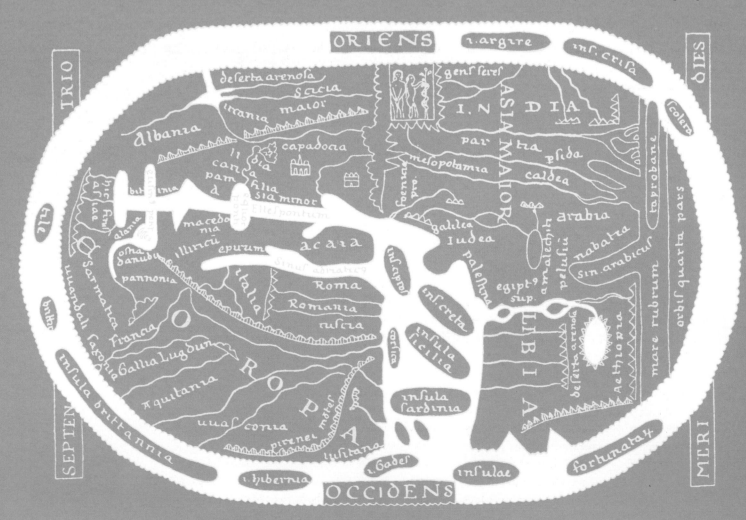

location for Eden. It is surely nonsensical to imagine that four rivers so far apart could emanate from a single source. But this is only with the benefit of modern knowledge. The ancient Greeks, for instance, believed that the waters of the fountain of Arethusa in Sicily started in the Peloponnese (southern Greece) and flowed all the way to Syracuse under the Ionian sea; so it would not have been difficult for them to credit the idea of a single subterranean stream with an enormously long course, feeding rivers that surfaced at places far away from one another in distant regions of the earth.

One theory concerning the Euphrates was that after meandering for a time among the marshes of southern Mesopotamia it actually ducked underground at that point, only to resurface hundreds of miles further south in the mountains of Ethiopia, where it was known as the Nile. Given such possibilities, the actual Eden might be almost anywhere in what was vaguely thought of as the East.

AN INACCESSIBLE EDEN

The snag was, of course, that nobody actually found this Eden. There were no tales of intrepid travelers returning with reports of failed attempts to clamber over insurmountable walls or of angels with flaming swords beating them back at the gate. One early writer to tackle this problem was the sixth-century Egyptian spice merchant Cosmas Indicopleustes who took early retirement to write a twelve-book treatise called *Christian Topography*. In this he proposed that up to the time of the Flood, all the earth's inhabitants lived in a relatively restricted zone not far from Eden itself. The effect of the Flood was to cut off this area from a large region of the earth that included the spot where Noah's ark eventually landed. These two land masses, he believed, were separated by a vast unnavigable ocean; yet they were still connected subterraneously by the four rivers of paradise, which flowed beneath the ocean only to resurface in various parts of the now inhabited world. This enabled him to maintain the continuing existence of paradise, and to find a place for it on his map, while at the same time asserting that it was now impossible for the inhabitants of our world ever to reach it.

An alternative explanation of the inaccessibility of paradise was based on an idea from Ezekiel: that it was situated at the top of a high mountain. Some writers suggested that the paradise mountain was so high that the waters of the Flood failed to reach it. Another writer, Honorius of Autun, put forward in his *De Imagine Mundi* (Concerning the Image of the World) the theory that paradise was surrounded by a wall of fire reaching to the sky while Peter Abelard, in his *Expositio in Hexaemeron* (Discussion of the Six Days), suggested that what made paradise unapproachable was not fire but a barrier of impenetrable darkness.

The English Benedictine Ralph (or Ranulphus) Higden included a chapter on paradise in his ambitious *Polychronicon*, which he planned as a history of the entire universe. Writing in the fourteenth century, he had no difficulty in believing in the existence of paradise—which, he asserted, must be as big as India or Egypt since, had it not been for the Fall, it would have had to be roomy enough to accommodate the whole human race.

PARADISE FOUND

The journals of Christopher Columbus prove that one did not have to be either an egghead theologian or an armchair historian to believe in the existence of paradise. On previous voyages Columbus had reached the Caribbean and got as close to the American continent as Haiti and the Dominican Republic, Cuba, and Puerto Rico. On his third voyage (1498), striking further south, he reached Trinidad, and on August 1 he had what was probably his first glimpse of the continent: what is now Venezuela. Over a fortnight later, he recorded the astonishing conviction that he had actually reached paradise. A number of observations supported this conclusion: the temperate climate, the delicious fruit, the golden ornaments he had seen the natives wearing, the lack of other islands along the coastline; above all the fact that his favorite book, D'Ailly's *Imago Mundi*, placed paradise at the first point of the Far East, where the sun rose on God's creation. The four rivers that his shipmates on the *Correo* had seen at the head of the gulf must be the Nile, the Euphrates, the Tigris, and the Ganges. Columbus, who never wavered from his certainty that he had reached the East Indies, thought that this was where Trinidad was: on the meridian. From various (mistaken) stellar observations he had also concluded that the earth was not round but shaped like a pear or, he thought, a round ball "on one part of which is placed something like a woman's breast." It was on the nipple of this breast that he located the earthly paradise.

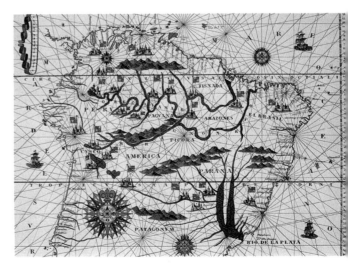

ABOVE: *The Amazon and the River Plate depicted on a 1582 Spanish map of South America. Venezuela is at the top of the map.*

THE MIDDLE AGES

ORIGINAL SIN

The most sinister spin-off from the Garden of Eden story is the strange doctrine of original sin, centered upon the puzzling assertion that all human beings, with only two exceptions (Christ and his mother), are riddled with sin and guilt even before they have drawn breath—because they are directly involved in the very first sin of all: the original sin, Adam's disobedience. This doctrine is both pernicious in its pessimistic view of human nature, and irrational, in its attribution of sin or guilt to unborn children.

It was this doctrine that ensured Adam and Eve a place in medieval art. At this time, art was predominantly religious and its main purpose was the teaching of the Christian message to a largely illiterate society. Radio and television were of course a long way off, but there were sermons aplenty, and lots of wonderful sacred music, and all over the churches and cathedrals (the only properly public buildings) could be seen wall-paintings, sculptures, and stained-glass windows illustrating the religious lessons. Adam and Eve had their part to play in reminding people of the origins of mankind's sinful condition. They even turned up among the misericords (carvings under the choir-stall seats, which, along with the gargoyles on the roof, gave skillful craftsmen scope to exercise the playful side of their talent). Not surprisingly, they also featured in the hesitant beginnings of the English theatrical tradition. *Adam* or *Le Mystère d'Adam*, composed in Norman French in the middle of the twelfth century, was an outstanding early example of what we now call mystery plays.

Challenging this conviction of the origin of human sinfulness is the curious fact that nothing in the Hebrew Bible lends it any support. In the words of an apocalyptic writing from the first century C.E., "every man is the Adam of his own soul": every man is his own (fallible) Adam; but while the view of humanity expressed in this saying may be fairly grim, it is not absurd. Both Jewish and Christian writers interpreted the Genesis story to mean that Adam brought death into the world, but even this inference, as we have seen, is hard to justify—so whoever dreamed up the idea of original sin?

BELOW: The Garden of Eden, from the Très Riches Heures *of the Duke of Berry (early 15th century). Garden of Eden scenes do not usually figure in Books of Hours. This one, painted separately by Pol de Limbourg, was inserted in the book just before the Annunciation scene on the facing page, so as to indicate the contrast between the old Adam and the new, whose coming is promised to Mary. Among the familiar paradise scenes the intricately designed fountain occupies a prominent place in the center.*

The short answer to this question is Saint Augustine. He had arguments in abundance, but the central conclusion on which he most relied was badly flawed, resting as it did on a misreading of Paul's letter to the Romans. What Paul said, writing in Greek, was this: "sin came into the world through one man and death through sin, and so death spread to all men." Then he adds a prepositional phrase which, translated literally, means "on top of which": "on top of which all men sinned"— each, evidently, through his own fault and of his own volition. But the Latin translation used by Augustine (who knew no Greek) reads *in quo*, which Augustine took to mean *in whom*. Who could Paul possibly be referring to? Why, to Adam, "the first man," now understood to have involved all mankind in his sinful act! How different the subsequent history of Christianity might have been without this one misunderstanding.

THE TREES OF PARADISE IN A NEW LIGHT

The tree of life in paradise is often associated with the cross of Christ. This is partly because the Greek word for the tree of life usually means wood or timber, sometimes a beam or post. So does the Latin; and Jerome, the author of the Vulgate, was clearly following the

Greek translation, not the Hebrew original. But the symbolism was not confined to the Latin tradition. The sixth-century Syriac *Book of the Cave of the Treasures* says of the tree of life in paradise that it "prefigured the redeeming cross, which is the veritable tree of life, and it was this that was fixed in the middle of the world." This is a stunning claim, appropriating on behalf of Christianity a deep-rooted mythology with a universal appeal.

The recurrent pattern of life/death/rebirth is common to virtually all religions. Christianity had already made a significant move by incorporating the third element of this dialectical triad, rebirth, in its teaching about resurrection. Death, the second element, was symbolized by the cross, which was at the heart of the gospel from the outset. The new typology, however, was a further conceptual advance, for now the cross itself came to be thought of as the source of new life, a tree whose branches spread their beneficent shade over the whole inhabited world. This symbolism is strikingly exhibited in a mosaic in the Roman basilica

of San Clemente, where the stylized vegetation of the world-tree spans heaven and earth in vine-like scrolls. Men, birds, and animals alike take refuge in its shade. Four streams issuing from the base of the tree/cross take up the theme of the four rivers of paradise, although their waters must now be understood as the water of life promised by Christ and no doubt also as the water of baptism. Immediately below the base of the tree stands the heavenly lamb of Revelation, with a nimbus round his head. On either side there are sheep gazing at him in adoration: this Lamb is also the Good Shepherd.

A further example of the rich iconographical potential of this theme is an eleventh-century miniature from Munich in which the Christ-figure almost grows out of the tree within the large central lozenge that occupies most of the page. He stretches out his arms to show that this tree is also a cross. With his left hand he grasps one of the branches, of which there are seven, recalling the Jewish seven-branched candlestick. In his outstretched right hand he holds a

ABOVE: The Garden of Paradise *by an unknown Rhenish master (c.1410). This very Christian garden is discussed at the foot of page 110.*

The Bad Apple

*H*ow did the "forbidden fruit" come to be identified as an apple? Part of the solution must lie in the fact that by the Middle Ages the word *pomum*, which in classical Latin simply meant any fruit from a tree, had come to bear the specific sense of an apple (hence French *pomme*, Italian *pomo*—*pomo vietato* being the Italian for what is called in English the "forbidden fruit"). But the word *malum*, which can only mean an apple, was also used as early as the ninth century, by Carolingian poets, to refer to the fruit of the forbidden tree. One of these poets (Audrad, a bishop) says that it was with an apple that the serpent tempted Eve; and another (Milo, a monk and a protégé of Charlemagne) writes in praise of Mary, the mother of Jesus, that having made reparation for Eve's sin in plucking the apple she reopened the gates of paradise.

Where did these poets find the apple? We do not really know; but suggestions include the Garden of the Hesperides and King Arthur's Avalon. The Garden of the Hesperides was located on the edge of the ocean in the extreme west; it could easily have been assimilated to the Fortunate Isles or the Isles of the Blessed that many Christian authors confused with paradise. This was where the daughters of the night guarded a tree that bore golden apples.

As for Avalon, the name comes from the Cornish word *aval*, meaning an apple. Geoffrey of Monmouth, in his *Life of Merlin*, identifies Avalon with the Fortunate Isles, generally located on the edge of the ocean, west of Cadiz Bay. But how the connection was made with paradise, or whether it was made at all, remains a mystery.

royal orb. This is close to the sun, which is placed just outside the central lozenge, as is the moon on the other side. Together sun and moon represent Christ's sovereignty over the entire universe. The traditional symbols of the four evangelists occupy the four corners, each supported by a female figure up to her waist in water, representing the four rivers of paradise. Another female figure at the center of the base performs the Atlas-like task of holding up the whole tree in which Christ is set and indicates the single original source from which the others flow. As in many of the earliest depictions of the crucifixion this Christ is a kingly figure, fully clothed. The proper response is not the pity that might be evoked by later pictures but awe and adoration.

Eden's other tree, bearing the forbidden fruit, is illustrated in a final example, also from Munich but painted more than three centuries later. Adam plays a subordinate role here, lying helplessly at the foot of the tree. On the right-hand side of the picture Eve, quite naked, takes an apple directly from the mouth of the serpent coiled round the tree and with her left hand offers another to people lining up to eat. A death's head grins evilly just above. On the other side Mary, the second Eve, clothed in her traditional blue but in the same pose as Eve and with the same gestures, offers fruit to a devout worshipper kneeling to receive it, while with her other hand she plucks an apple from the tree, just below a miniature Christ who is hanging on a cross set in the middle of the tree's abundant foliage.

A GARDEN ENCLOSED

"A garden enclosed is my sister, my spouse; a spring shut up, a fountain sealed. Thy plants are an orchard of pomegranates, with pleasant fruits; camphire, with spikenard, spikenard and saffron; calamus and cinnamon, with all trees of frankincense; myrrh and aloes, with all the chief spices: a fountain of gardens, a well of living waters, and streams from Lebanon."

This quotation comes from the Song of Solomon, a love song addressed to a girl whose virginal state is expressed in three telling metaphors. Admitted into the Hebrew Bible on the pretense that it was really a song of God"s love for his people, it became a favorite text among the Fathers of the Christian church, no less adept than the rabbis at reading spiritual meanings into words originally directed to a very different purpose. The numerous interpretations of the enclosed garden include virginity, the Christian soul, a clear conscience, the whole church (watered by the four rivers of the gospel), the heavenly Jerusalem, and the monastic cloister— the one we will focus on here.

All monasteries had gardens. At some point the monks began to surround these with pillared porticoes or arcades. Most cloisters are square in shape, and many have a fountain in the middle, signifying the single source flowing out of Eden. The four sides of the cloister could represent the four rivers of Eden, the four gospels, and much else besides.

Bernard of Clairvaux, the most influential of all twelfth-century Christian writers, conceived the cloister to be "a paradise protected by the rampart of the monastic rule." Thus the image of the rampart found its way into a number of striking representations of paradise, including a very well-known painting (attributed to an unnamed Rhenish master) of a garden surrounded by a crenellated wall (*see page 109*). In the center of the picture a lady is quietly reading a book, and a baby at her feet is playing a zither held for him by another lady. A third woman is ladling water from a well. A winged figure talking to an armored knight in one corner proves that this is no ordinary garden, but is in fact the garden of paradise: the central figure is Mary, the baby is Jesus, the angel is Michael, the armored knight is Saint George, and the lady with the zither is Saint Cecilia, patron saint of all musicians. Even the flowers have symbolic meanings.

Finally, by an extraordinary twist, the walled rampart is transferred to the original Garden of Eden, which is occasionally portrayed as situated in a castle courtyard that carries with it the sense of the enclosed garden.

POETIC LICENSE

EPHRAEM

A huge number of Christian poets have tackled the subject of paradise; the least-known of the outstanding three or four is the fourth-century Syriac poet Saint Ephraem. Ephraem visualized paradise as a conically shaped mountain surrounding the earth-encircling ocean and including our sky within it—so that it rises above the earth and yet also envelops it. The hymn below is an example of his work.

> There came to my ear
> from the Scripture which had been read
> a word which caused me joy
> on the subject of the Thief;
> it gave comfort to my soul
> amidst the multitude of its vices,
> telling how He had compassion on the Thief.
> O may He bring me too
> into that Garden at the sound of whose name
> I am overwhelmed with joy;
> my mind bursts its reins
> as it goes forth to contemplate Him.

This hymn follows up the theme of the good thief, with a familiar association:

> Adam was heedless
> as guardian of Paradise,
> for the crafty thief
> stealthily entered;
> leaving aside the fruit
> —which most men would covet—
> he stole instead
> the Garden's inhabitant.
> Adam's Lord came out to seek him;
> He entered Sheol and found him there,
> then led and brought him out
> to set him once more in Paradise.

The last stanza pictures the souls of the just waiting patiently for "the bodies they love," so that when the gate of paradise is eventually opened, the souls, united with their bodies, might join in praising him who rescued Adam from Sheol and led him, along with so many others, into paradise. Elsewhere in this series of hymns, Ephraem mentions Noah, Moses, Jacob, Joseph, Samson, David, Job, and Jeremiah. Like Adam, they all had to wait on the outskirts of hell until freed by their Redeemer.

DANTE

As the best known and most influential of all Christian poets, Dante must be included in any search for the Christian paradise, for the heavenly paradise is the theme and title of the last of the three parts of his great poem *Commedia*. The earthly paradise, on the other hand, takes up only a single canto.

Dante believed that the earth was a globe. The inhabited part was confined to the northern hemisphere; the southern hemisphere was inaccessible. When Satan was hurled down from heaven, the force of his fall carried him right through the earth into its very center, where he now resides. His fall also caused an enormous upheaval in the southern hemisphere: it resulted in the creation of a mountain, Mount Purgatory, on the other side of the earth directly opposite Jerusalem. Dante's most startlingly contribution to the myth of the earthly paradise was to locate it on the summit of this mountain.

Having left hell via a winding path from the center of the earth that took them directly southward, the travelers reach the surface again at the foot of Mount Purgatory. They immediately begin to climb. Upon reaching the summit, Dante becomes aware that he is now in the Garden of Eden, the earthly paradise. This is fully described: it has a fountain, but only two rivers rather than four: the rivers of forgetfulness and remembrance.

BELOW: Dante and Virgil on the threshold of Limbo, from a 14th-century manuscript in the Biblioteca Nazionale Marciana in Venice. At the end of the Inferno, the first part of the Commedia, *Dante is led by Virgil to Limbo, where the pair will be greeted by the souls of good people who, having died before the coming of Christ, were never baptized and so cannot get to heaven. Described by Dante as a castle set within a garden, Limbo foreshadows the heavenly Jerusalem, a walled city inside a garden.*

This canto, the twenty-eighth, concludes with an evocation of the classical legend: "those who in olden times sang of the age of gold and its happy state dreamed of this place." Dante was convinced that the only people who could enter paradise, even the earthly paradise, were those who accepted Christ—either formally, as Christian believers, or, before his coming, by way of hope and expectation. But all the members of the second group, which is composed of figures from the Old Testament (Adam and Eve, Moses, Rachel, Sarah, Rebekah, Judith, and Ruth), are now in the true, heavenly paradise and Dante will meet all of them.

Leaving the earth, the poet finds himself immediately in heaven. Now his task is to pass through each of the rings of heaven, each of which is presided over by a heavenly body. The further out he travels, the faster he finds the rings revolve. When he reaches the tenth heaven, the outermost ring that encloses the rest, he finds that its center is motionless: this is the Empyrean, the very mind of God himself. Although in one sense, therefore, the journey through paradise consists of an ascent, in another more important sense it represents a deepening understanding of spiritual realities.

In the third and final section of the *Divine Comedy*, Paradiso, the garden theme returns just once. Beatrice, Dante's guide at this point, turns to him somewhat reproachfully and says: "Why does my face so fill you with love that you do not look rather to the fair garden

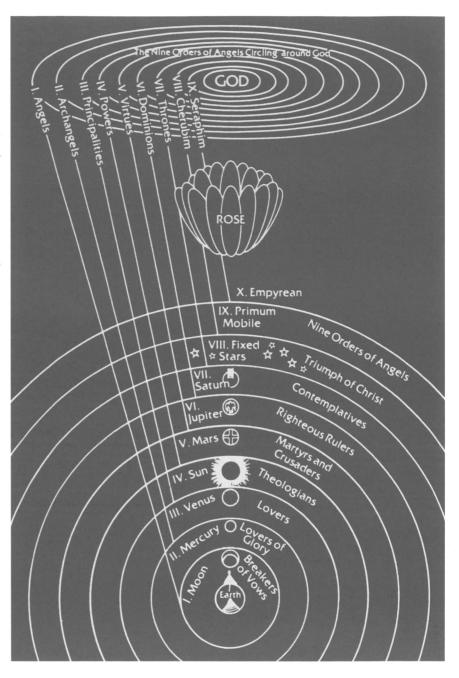

The Paradise of George Herbert

*T*he seventeenth-century religious poet George Herbert, with a characteristic blend of piety and wit, successfully interiorizes the paradise theme in a poem with that title:

I bless thee, Lord, because I GROW
Among thy trees, which in a ROW
To thee both fruit and order OW.

What open force, or hidden CHARM,
Can blast my fruit, or bring me HARM,
When the inclosure is thine ARM.

Inclose me still for fear I START,
Be to me rather sharp and TART,
Than let me want thy hand and ART.

When thou dost greater judgements SPARE,
And with thy knife but prune and PARE,
Ev'n fruitful trees more fruitful ARE.

Such sharpness shows the sweetest FREND:
Such cuttings rather heal than REND:
And such beginnings touch their END.

that blossoms beneath the rays of Christ? Here is the Rose wherein the Divine Word became flesh; here are the sweet-smelling lilies who took the right path." The Rose is the Virgin Mary; the lilies are the blessed in heaven; the garden is heaven itself. Another rose, the last in the poem, is an even more important symbol: "Into the yellow of the eternal rose, which rises in ranks and expands and breathes forth a scent of praise to the sun that makes perpetual spring, Beatrice drew me. She said, 'Behold how great the assembly of the white robes! See our city, how wide is its circuit! See our seats so filled that there is now room for only a few more souls!'" This rose is the whole of the population of the heavenly city. Its spreading petals form a kind of amphitheater in which the rows of the blessed are seated. At this culminating point of his poem Dante

ABOVE: *The Universe of Dante. c. 1300. Dante Alighieri, The Divine Comedy. Vol.3. Paradise. In Dante's universe, as in Aristotle's, there were seven planets, including the sun and the moon, that revolved round the earth. The outermost circle was made up of the fixed stars. Beyond these was the Empyrean.*

manages to combine, in the single beautiful image of the rose, the two central images of the last chapter of Revelation: the garden and the city. Here, surely, is the quintessence of the paradise theme.

MILTON

With Milton, writing 300 years or so after Dante, we enter a different world. Although he too is a Christian writer, as well-versed in classical lore as Dante himself, and acquainted with many of the legends relating to the Eden tradition, his approach to the subject could hardly be more different. Milton's qualities are those of a novelist or tragedian, and *Paradise Lost* was first conceived not as an epic, which is what it later became, but as a tragedy. The poet projects upon the story his own conception of the psychological struggles between all the characters involved: God himself, Satan and his hellish lieutenants (Beelzebub, Belial, Moloc, and the rest), Adam and Eve and the named angels. The encounters of Satan with Adam and Eve, and of the human couple with one another, are treated with great finesse.

The opening of the poem, Milton's summary of the story that is to follow, could not be more traditional:

> *Of man's first disobedience, and the fruit*
> *Of that forbidden tree, whose mortal taste*
> *Brought death into the world, and all our woe,*
> *With loss of Eden, till one greater man*
> *Restore us, and regain the blissful seat*
> *Sing heavenly Muse.*

But this is just the prelude. Genesis deals with the story of Adam and Eve in a few pages; Milton needs hundreds: twelve books, many of them over a thousand lines long. So it is no surprise that he greatly expands this tale of mutual recrimination.

He does not doubt that Adam led Eve ("blushing like the morn") to what he calls "the nuptial bower" immediately after he had been smitten by her beauty. For she herself had approached him:

> *Led by her heavenly maker, though unseen,*
> *Nor uninformed of nuptial sanctity and marriage rites.*

Talking to the angel Raphael, Adam admits to having felt stirrings of passion for the first time in his short life:

> *Commotion strange, in all enjoyments else*
> *Superior and unproved, here only weak*
> *Against the charm of beauty's powerful glance.*

Being in love, Adam thought that everything Eve said or desired was the "wisest, virtuous, discreetest, best." Hearing this, Raphael warns him not to go too far:

> *In loving thou dost well, in passion not*
> *Wherein true love consists not…*

So he should take heed "lest passion sway thy judgement to do aught, which else free will would not admit." We might suppose on reading this that when Adam eventually succumbed to Eve's blandishments, it would be as a consequence of being blinded by passion. On the contrary, he did so "against his better knowledge, not deceived." It was just that he could not bear the thought of losing her: "to lose thee," he tells her, "were to lose my self."

According to Milton's conception, it was the actual act of disobedience that changed everything. Both Adam and Eve were immediately inflamed with carnal desire: "in lust they burn." Adam feels ashamed:

> *Of honor void*
> *Of innocence, of faith, of purity,*
> *Our wonted ornaments now soiled and stained,*
> *And in our faces evident the signs*
> *Of foul concupiscence.*

Foul concupiscence? Because he had just made love to his own wife? Apparently so. Milton, the last great Christian poet to treat the theme of paradise, was a true Puritan.

MECHTILD OF MAGDEBURG

*G*enuine mystics are rare, a tiny fraction of the human race. But musical geniuses are equally rare, so rarity alone is not enough to justify outright skepticism in the face of descriptions of visions and revelations. Wary respect would be a more appropriate response.

Mechtild of Magdeburg, a nun who was born around 1207 and died around 1282, wrote of her experiences of ecstasy and rapture in *The Flowing Light of the Godhead*. This book, whose title was revealed to her by God, was composed over a period of more than 20 years. The experiences of any mystic are not merely colored by their cultural context, but controlled and determined by it. In Mechtild's case, the determining factors were primarily her Christian faith and education, but there is no doubt that she was also influenced by medieval conventions of courtly love.

The conventions of courtly love arose out of and in reaction to the stifling realities of married life. Marriage in those days was largely a transaction, and loveless marriages were the norm. The conviction that true love, being impossible within marriage, must be sought outside of it led in two directions. One was adultery: hence the legend of Tristan and Isolde, and the story of the liaison between Guinevere, King Arthur's queen, and the knight Sir Lancelot. The other direction was a kind of idealized and etherealized sex. Any consummation of this ideal love is barred; quite acceptable, however, are clandestine meetings in which the lovers swear undying allegiance to each other and exchange a chaste kiss.

In one of Mechtild's visions heaven appeared as a bridal chamber into which Christ the Son of God occasionally admitted holy women who had pledged themselves to lifelong virginity in the service of God. In another, one of her most remarkable visions, she pictures herself as a noble lady in love with a handsome youth. The lady, she makes clear, is her own soul; the youth is Christ: "Fair youth, I long for you. Where shall I find you?" After a number of disappointments, he invites her to meet "the Son of the virgin": "Come at noontime to the shade of the spring, to the bed of love. There in the coolness you shall refresh yourself with him." Before the meeting she dons the slip of humility, the dress of chastity, and the cloak of her good name. She approaches him nervously: "What do you bid me, Lord?" "Take off your clothes." "Lord, what will happen to me then?" He explains that the clothes he has told her to put aside are those of "fear and shame and all external virtues." She complies, but is nervous still: "Lord, I am a naked soul, and you are in yourself a well-adorned God."

Following this protestation, there is a brief but unforgettable moment of blissful union. Mechtild does not shrink from recounting this: "Then a blessed stillness that both desire comes over them. He surrenders himself to her and she surrenders herself to him."

RIGHT: Gianlorenzo Bernini (1598-1680) carved the Ecstasy or Rapture of Saint Theresa, the famous Carmelite nun from Avila, in Spain, for the church of Santa Maria della Vittoria in Rome, a few years after her canonization in 1622. Though in Mechtild's case there was no angel armed with the dart of divine love, her experience must have closely resembled the one so evocatively portrayed by Bernini.

DOWN TO EARTH

So powerful and pervasive was the influence of the Church in medieval Europe that one might be forgiven for thinking that this was all there was. The Christian story, which begins in paradise, retained its fascination—especially for artists—throughout the Renaissance.

To be convinced of this it is enough to take a stroll through any western museum or art gallery. Yet even in the Middle Ages society was not entirely church-ridden. This was the age of chivalry, also therefore of romances and love-songs. Legendary tales with a paradisaical setting were subject to other influences too, some of them dating back to Late Antiquity. What is more, some of the gardens described in stories or portrayed in pictures were very earthy indeed.

LEFT: The Garden of Earthly Delights, Hieronymus Bosch (1450-1516). Central panel of a triptych.

MEDIEVAL GARDENS

ARCADIA

The Golden Age, the Elysian Fields, the Isles of the Blessed: all these legends retained their influence throughout the medieval period. To these legendary places another must now be added: Arcadia. Geographically speaking, Arcadia is a mountainous region in southern Greece; its importance for paradise is that it is the name selected by the Roman poet Virgil for the idyllic spot in which the young lovers he writes about in his first published book, the *Eclogues*, conducted their amorous encounters.

Virgil's model for this collection of pastoral poems was the so-called *Idylls* of the Greek poet Theocritus (first half of the third century B.C.E. Theocritus lived in Sicily, which is where he set his poems, charming little stories of shepherds and shepherdesses languishing with love, and dwelling in pleasant country places with grassy banks decked with flowers of all colors, rippling brooks, singing birds, and above all plenty of cool shade in which to seek relief from the Mediterranean

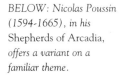

BELOW: Nicolas Poussin (1594-1665), in his Shepherds of Arcadia, *offers a variant on a familiar theme.*

sun. But by the time Virgil was writing, over two centuries later, the Roman province of Sicily had an every-day feel to it. Searching for something more exotic, Virgil turned instead not to the real Arcadia (which he never saw), but to a fictive paradisaical spot where his heroes and heroines led lives of an implausible rustic simplicity. The new Arcadia kept its place in the European imagination long afterward. Even the names Virgil borrowed from Theocritus keep reappearing: centuries later John Milton, taking over the pastoral genre in his *Lycidas*, is still asking himself,

> Were it not better as others use,
> To sport with Amaryllis in the shade?

Having begun her long and literally shady career in Theocritus' *Idylls*, Amaryllis continues it in Virgil's *Eclogues*, and hears herself invoked once again in Milton's pastoral elegy.

The influences of Homer, Theocritus, and Virgil, combined to give later poets an ideal landscape of forest and flowery meadow. At the end of the twelfth century André Le Chapelain describes in his *De Amore*

an enchanting garden dedicated to the god of love: this contains a fountain of pure water and a great tree whose branches provide shade all around. The essential nature of Arcadia may be conveyed by an old English word, long fallen into disuse: the word pleasance. It sums up a tradition of an ideal landscape that owed nothing at all to Christian notions of paradise.

In the early sixteenth century the Neapolitan writer Sannazaro succeeded in reviving the popularity of Arcadia as a theme of both prose and poetry. He and his followers (one of them was Sir Philip Sidney) all speak of paradise. But their subject is no longer man's relationship to God: it is human love.

A last ironic reflection on Arcadia is to be found in a famous painting of Poussin (1594–1665) that portrays a lady gazing enigmatically at three shepherds gathered round a tombstone. One of them is pointing to the inscription. The picture bears the caption "*Et in Arcadia ego.*" Death is speaking: "I am present even in Arcadia."

THE ROMANCE OF THE ROSE

On the first page of *Le Roman de la Rose*, the most celebrated and influential of all medieval romances, there is a description of the countryside in May that shows how much its author, Guillaume de Lorris, writing in the first half of the thirteenth century, has borrowed from Arcadia. The dry woods are once more coming into leaf, the earth, forgetting the miseries of winter, is putting on a new dress, the birds are singing sweetly: "it is then that young men must seek love and merriment in the fair, mild weather."

But *Le Roman de la Rose* is much more than a pastoral idyll: it combines a number of quite different genres. First, as its name suggests, it is a romance. Like all romances it is the story of a quest—in this instance the quest for a beautiful rose, spotted by the youthful poet (20 years old, he tells us in the first line of the poem) in a garden to which he has contrived to gain admittance. Secondly, after naming his poem Guillaume tells us that in it is contained (*enclose*) "the whole art of love." (There may be an intentional allusion here to the theme of the enclosed garden.) Besides being a romance it is a love manual in the tradition of Ovid's *The Art Of Love*. In the third place the poem is a lyric: the love so eloquently expressed and described in the poem is that of the narrator himself, and in the act of giving voice to his love he is drawing upon the traditions of courtly love that had found expression in the songs of the troubadours in southern France during the preceding century.

The lady to whom the poem is addressed "is so precious and worthy of love that she should be called

Rose"; so in recounting his efforts to reach and obtain the beautiful rose he has glimpsed in the garden the narrator is giving a very obvious hint that his allegorical story should be read as a lyrical love-song. As in the songs of the troubadours which had inspired him, the poet's love is never consummated; and this part of the tale ends with a sense of loss, a loss "so great and so apparent" that, Guillaume suspects, "the fear and distress I suffer will result in my death."

BACKWARD AND FORWARD

Guillaume de Lorris' work in *Le Roman de la Rose* is both the last fine flowering of a centuries-old tradition and the anticipation of what is to come. The garden it describes is unquestionably paradise, even though the coveted prize inside its walls is not an apple but a rose: like the original "enclosed garden" of the Song of

ABOVE: *This picture from a 16th-century illustrated edition of* Le Roman de la Rose *shows the lover as he is at last being admitted into the rose garden by the fair Oiseuse (Leisure).*

Aucassin and Nicolette

*W*ritten about the same time (c. 1225) as *Le Roman de la Rose*, the anonymous story (part verse, part prose) of Aucassin and Nicolette is best seen an ironical reflection on the same traditions and the same genres. The result is a kind of topsy-turvy universe in which the story revolves round the efforts of Nicolette to overcome all the obstacles that keep her apart from her beloved Aucassin. On one occasion she guides him to her hiding-place in the forest by means of a series of encoded messages that both reveal and conceal her location and identity. On another she escapes from imprisonment in Spain and makes her way to Aucassin's castle in France disguised as a troubadour.

So although the prologue to the poem announces a traditional tale of how young love surmounts all the obstacles in its way, it also hints that most of the chivalry and prowess will be displayed not by the noble Aucassin but by the valiant Nicolette (Nicolette *la prous*). And in fact this is how it turns out. The traditional tale of the chivalrous lover's search for his beloved is subverted into one in which the real heroism and resourcefulness is on the side of the woman.

RENAISSANCE GARDENS AND FOUNTAINS

THE FOUNTAIN OF YOUTH

Although the waters of the fountain of youth seem to mingle easily with the waters of eternal life they spring from a different source. The association of water with life is universal; in the Bible it is a gift of God, and in the Gospel of John Jesus identifies himself as a source of living water, that is to say of everlasting life. The river of living water flowing from the throne of God in the last chapter of the Book of Revelation also promises eternal life. The very different legend of the fountain of youth, on the other hand, by which is meant an endless source of continual rejuvenation, is not Semitic but Indian. Found in the writings of the

Songs it represents the state of virginity. At first the rose is completely hidden, and the garden is approached from the outside. Even after gaining entrance the young lover is confronted by a hedge surrounding the plot in which the rose herself will eventually be seen.

Much of the piquancy of this love story about an enclosed garden, however, derives from the religious meanings it evokes: the monastic cloister and the church. But this garden was also a frequent symbol of the Virgin Mary. In the sixteenth-century "Litany of Loreto" she is called upon by a whole series of names. "Enclosed garden" is one of them. "Mystical Rose" is another. In both medieval and renaissance art she is of course portrayed most often as the Virgin Mother, and one variation of this theme is set in a rose garden, this combining the twin symbols of garden and rose in a single picture.

Guillaume de Lorris' 4,000-line romance is less than a fifth of the whole poem now known as *Le Roman de la Rose*; 40 years later Jean de Meung, a poet with a very different conception of love, grafted onto it a lengthy extension whose final pages recount in detail the literal deflowering of the rose. His addition, though skillfully written, meant that the poem that opened with delicately allegorical hints ends with a series of suggestive nudges, and ensured that it would be read by future generations in a much earthier fashion. The paradise theme had not lost its potency, but its religious significance was already fading.

RIGHT: The Fountain of Eternal Youth illustrated in the 15th-century De Sphaera manuscript, which is in the Biblioteca Estense of Modena.

early Brahmans, it was only very much later that it gained a place in European literature.

Its first appearance there is in the Epistle of Prester John (c.1165; "Prester" is an abbreviation of "Presbyter"—priest). This spoof letter was one the most successful hoaxes in history. Now universally recognized as spurious, it rapidly gained credence, and a dozen or so years later (1177) Pope Alexander III wrote a letter to its totally fictitious author, who claimed to have gained control over an enormous kingdom in the East. (According to one account it would take four months to march across it.) The bogus Epistle gives a full description of Prester John's territory. Among other marvels it contained a forest located at the foot of Mount Olympus. From the forest flowed a spring whose waters then ran close to the earthly paradise and whose fragrance combined the scents of all the spices. Whoever drank three times from the water while fasting would never fall sick and would continue throughout life with the appearance of a man or woman of 32.

In the second half of the thirteenth century the kingdom of Prester John is described in the travel writings of Marco Polo, and a century later Sir John Mandeville (Jehan de Mandeville) testified to the durability of the legend in *The Voiage and Travayle of Sir John Maundeville*, speaking for instance of "a great flood that comes from Paradise, and it is full of precious stones, and no drop of water, and it runs with great waves into the gravelly sea." Another fountain of youth appears in the fifteenth-century story of Huon de Bordeaux, who is said to have discovered it somewhere

BELOW: Marco Polo setting out with his uncles from Venice for the Far East. From a late 14th-century manuscript of Travels of Marco Polo (The Book of the Grand Khan). *This was one of the works that gave Christopher Columbus the urge to cross the Atlantic in search of the Indies.*

near the Persian Gulf. After bathing in the fountain he felt immediately refreshed and although previously exhausted by his recent labors, he recovered all his pristine vigor.

A rather different legend became attached to the name of Ponce de León, the discoverer of Florida, who, like Columbus, believed that he had landed in the true Indies. Encouraged by the stories of the native Indians, he went in search of a mysterious fountain of youth—and it is sometimes claimed that he actually found it.

Nor is there any shortage of pictorial evidence. Hieronymus Bosch's paintings, for example, show that somehow or other a fountain had found its way into the Garden of Eden itself (as well as into the Garden of Earthly Delights). Lucas Cranach (1472–1523) painted a vivid representation of a scene that shows the sick, the elderly and the crippled being carried on carts, wheelbarrows, and stretchers, and even on men's backs, to the edge of a life-giving pool. They emerge healed, happy, rejuvenated. The lowering cliffs on the left contrast with a smiling landscape on the right.

THE GARDEN OF EARTHLY DELIGHTS

Although Hieronymus Bosch includes a picture of the Garden of Eden in what is probably his best-known work (it is the left-hand panel of the triptych shown below) this is named after the subject of the central panel, the Garden of Earthly Delights. "Garden of Delights," *hortus deliciarum*, is the literal translation of the Hebrew Garden of Eden, as Bosch must have known. Bosch (c.1450–1516) was a contemporary of Leonardo da Vinci and a prominent representative of what we now call the Northern Renaissance, yet he was scarcely typical of this; nor do the grotesque images that both fascinated and appalled his contemporaries owe anything to his great Flemish predecessors though they may well owe something to Marco Polo's description of the paradise enjoyed by the rather dubious character he called "The Old Man of the Mountain.")

The pictures that best illustrate the enormous distance between Bosch's bizarre conception of paradise and the traditional image of a tranquil garden scene are *The Haywain* and *The Garden of Earthly Delights*. (Bosch was the favorite painter of Philip II of Spain, another orthodox Catholic with a predilection for the macabre; which explains why both of these pictures now hang in the Prado in Madrid.) These canvases are best known for the central panels that give them their names. Yet since each of these is flanked by a picture of the

Sailing to Byzantium

Soon after Islam had emerged in the seventh century as a powerful new religious force the "paradises" of the kings of Persia became transformed into desirable orchards that made havens of refuge for the parched inhabitants of the Arabian deserts. The home of Allah himself, the seventh heaven, was an orchard. Beautiful gardens were planted all the way from Baghdad in Mesopotamia to Granada in Spain, and gardens are frequently evoked in *The Thousand and One Nights*. The design of the garden of Harun-al-Rashid in Baghdad included a circular basin with a silver tree in the middle and mechanical birds chirping and fidgeting on its branches. This was imitated in Christian Constantinople, as the poet Yeats recalls in his poem Sailing to Byzantium (Byzantium, the city's earlier name, has a more magical sound):

> Once out of nature I shall never take
> My bodily form from any natural thing,
> But such a form as Grecian goldsmiths make
> Of hammered gold and gold enamelling
> To keep a drowsy Emperor awake;
> Or set upon a golden bough to sing
> To lords and ladies of Byzantium
> Of what is past, or passing, or to come.

ABOVE: *Persian miniature of a paradise garden with flowering trees and a refreshing stream, c.1300.*

Garden of Eden, Bosch clearly intends the viewer to link the two scenes and also no doubt to recognize that the strange goings-on of the figures in the central panels are connected with the portentous event exhibited on their left. As the viewer's gaze shifts eventually to the right-hand panel, what comes into view is a savage depiction of hell that graphically displays the even grimmer consequences of the activities shown or symbolized in the center.

In the middle section of *The Garden of Earthly Delights* naked women frolic in a circular pool, while a large number of men circle round them, riding horses or, in one case, a strange creature with the head of a bird of prey. At the left side of the pool a woman with an apple on her head peers over the edge and other women look interestedly out at the naked male riders.

Above these, there is another pool with a huge globe in the middle supporting a peculiar column that also acts as a fountain. On a rim encircling the globe are three human couples in different postures. The pair in the middle are performing an acrobatic handstand, taking no notice of the couple on their left, who look suspiciously like Adam and Eve.

The bottom third of the picture, the weirdest of all, is flanked on the left by an owl perched beside a sea-plant with a sinister fruit consisting of a bubble with a pair of lovers inside. On the right there is another owl, a symbol of knowledge but also of evil, crouching on top of a strange headless creature with four arms and four legs, recognizably human. There are no children in this picture, and all the adults are either greedy, lazy, lustful, or vain.

BELOW: The Garden of Earthly Delights by Hieronymus Bosch (1450-1516). This picture is discussed in the text, left.

THE LAND OF COCKAIGNE

The Land of Cockaigne offers a particularly ironic version of the paradise theme. Cockaigne, above all else, is a land of (improbable) plenty, in which food and drink of every description is available for the asking. Like so many of the themes associated with paradise, this idea is first found in Greek Antiquity. In what may well be the first cookery book ever written, the *Deipnosophists* (Learned Banquet), Athenaeus of Naucratis (who was writing around 200 C.E.) compiled a number of quotations from earlier Greek sources that relate to fabulous banquets. One of these is from *The Miners of Pherecrates*, where one of the characters recalls a meal during which, among other marvels, "roast thrushes, dressed for a rechauffé, flew round our mouths entreating us to swallow them as we lay stretched among the myrtles and anemones."

Curiously reminiscent of this is a passage from an early English (or, in this case Anglo-Irish) satirical poem called The Land of Cockaigne (c.1305), which begins:

> Far out to sea to the west of Spain
> There is a land that is called Cokaygne.

And continues:

> Paradise, true, may be merry and bright
> But the Land of Cokaygne is a fairer sight.

(Among other allusions to paradise in this poem is a mention of the presence of Elijah and Enoch.) This Cockaigne, exceptionally, is located in an abbey—probably modeled on the Gray Abbey in Kildare, County Down, for Kildare figures in the title of the collection. The main emphasis, however, is on food. Among the innumerable birds that sing ceaselessly day and night are roasted geese:

> Geese that have been roasted on a spit
> Fly to that abbey—I swear by God—
> Crying out loud: Geese, all hot, all hot.

In early-fourteenth-century Ulster, no doubt, roast goose was thought of as more of a luxury than roast thrush. In other descriptions of this earthly paradise the rivers flow with wine, the houses are constructed out of cake and barley-sugar, the streets are paved with pastry, and the shops supply goods without charge. In one account buttered larks fall from the sky like manna.

Versions of the same theme occur in many languages: Spanish, French and German (*Schlaraffenland*, associated with the name of Hans Sachs, of Meistersinger fame), and finally Dutch, which was no doubt where the Flemish artist Pieter Bruegel (c.1525–69) got the idea for his great picture. Having indulged themselves unstintingly in all the goodies of Schlaraffenland, the people he portrays are now suffering the consequences. If this were a scene from a present-day picture they would probably be assumed to be recuperating from a visit to the Land of Cocaine.

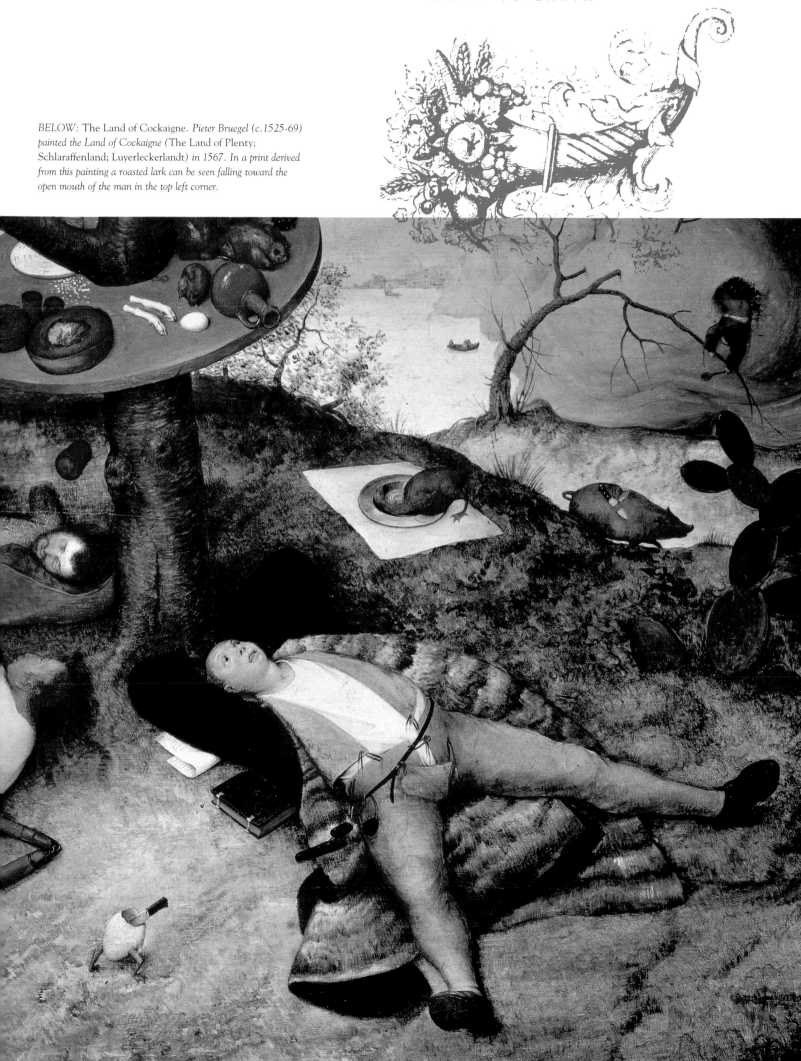

BELOW: The Land of Cockaigne. *Pieter Bruegel (c.1525-69) painted the Land of Cockaigne (The Land of Plenty; Schlaraffenland; Luyerleckerlandt) in 1567. In a print derived from this painting a roasted lark can be seen falling toward the open mouth of the man in the top left corner.*

*R*omantic tales about the travels of Alexander the Great enjoyed an extraordinary popularity in the Middle Ages. The story of his journey to Paradise is of Jewish origin, dating back probably to the Talmudic era, around 500 C.E.

Nearing the end of his journey eastwards, Alexander reached an extremely wide river whose name, he learned, was the Ganges, "whose source is the paradise of joy." Eager to earn "a share of this joy," he planned a major expedition, with 500 men and enough food to last the summer. After sailing upstream for over a month, struggling against the current and buffeted by heavy winds, he spied in the distance what looked like a city wall, amazingly high and absolutely smooth. It took three more days' sailing along the side of this wall before someone spotted a tiny crevice in a fortified window.

Immediately Alexander dispatched a squad of men in a skiff to demand tribute from the inhabitants of the city. A man appeared at the window and greeted them politely. Unmoved by their threats, he offered the envoys a gift for their king, a gemstone the size and shape of a human eye. This was the wonderstone. However the king regards it, he said, either as a gift or as tribute, it will have the effect of putting an end to his greed.

Abandoning the expedition, Alexander returned to Susa, where he summoned the wisest men among the Jews and gentiles and asked them to explain to him the mystery of the gemstone. They all confessed themselves baffled, but on hearing the story a wise old Jew named Papas asked to see the king. Alexander, "who both liked and desired conversations with old men," told him of his expedition to paradise. Papas was amazed, and told him he was lucky to escape with his life. When he saw the stone he asked for a scale to be fetched, and a pound of gold. The stone easily outweighed the gold, and however much gold was added to the pan it made no difference.

Then, however, Papas sprinkled dust over the stone, which immediately became lighter than a feather. Alexander still did not understand, so Papas explained. The stone is his eye, heavy with ambition and greed, as heavy as everything he covets. Now, covered with the dust of death, it weighs nothing. That is also the true worth of his greedy eye. When he is dead and buried, covered with the dust of the earth, it too will have no weight and no value.

Alexander rewards Papas for his wise counsel, takes the lesson of the wonderstone to heart, and ends his career of conquest. Having traced the water of life (the Ganges) to its source (paradise), where he received the gift of understanding (the wonderstone), he can end his days in peace and virtue.

RIGHT: Alexander the Great (356-323 B.C.E.). A 14th-century carving of Alexander the Great's ascension to heaven, which appears in the Byzantine church of Peribleptos in Mistra, Greece.

OTHER

Although the idea of what it is to be human varies widely from society to society, all religions share a common concern in their preoccupation with death. The yearning to reach beyond this mortal existence toward the eternal and the absolute is articulated in many different ways, be it in the desire to return to the rhythms of nature, the search for harmony with the universe, absorption into the invisible spirit world, or the expectation of reincarnation.

WORLDS

UTOPIAS

"UTOPIA" IS A WORD THAT NOW MEANS ROUGHLY THE SAME AS "PARADISE." ASKED TO SAY HOW WE ENVISAGE PARADISE MOST OF US WOULD RESPOND BY DESCRIBING UTOPIA, AND VICE VERSA: A PLACE WHERE EVERYTHING IS AS IT SHOULD BE (OR HOW WE WOULD LIKE IT TO BE).

Chapter

9

Thomas More used the word "utopia" in the sixteenth century as the title of a book in which he imagined a voyage to a country governed on ideal principles. The word at this time simply meant "nowhere," but it quickly came to mean an ideal world, the imagined realization of unattainable longings. People interested in the concept of utopia often contrast it with dystopia, by which they generally mean the worst, as opposed to the best, of all possible worlds—the terrible actualization of a frightening nightmare. But it proves surprisingly easy to pass from the best to the worst.

LEFT: In foretelling a new era of absolute peace and harmony the prophet Isaiah had predicted that "the wolf shall dwell with the lamb" (Isaiah 11:6). The smug expression of Andrew Murray's lamb shows that she is quite satisfied with a lion instead.

UTOPIAN PARADISE

PRIVATE UTOPIAS

PAST AND PRIVATE

As long as the majority of people still believed in the continued existence of an earthly paradise (the lost Garden of Eden) then this, if they searched for an ideal place at all, is what they hoped to find. We know that Christopher Columbus thought he *had* found it: for him and people of his time it was not "nowhere" but a real place. But as geographical knowledge increased, the hope of finding paradise as a place literally existing on earth dwindled away and was replaced by a belief in paradise as a spiritual—heavenly—place, or by thoughts of a private utopia—each individual's consciously imagined ideal world, which can never be realized.

The first paradise, the Garden of Eden, was depicted in the Bible as incomplete without a man to inhabit it, and, once the man had been created, still incomplete without a woman. The pair lived for a time (a little over six hours is what Adam told Dante when interrogated on the subject on Mount Purgatory) in complete harmony; then trouble arose with the eating of the forbidden fruit. One lesson that we are perhaps meant to draw from the story is that the actual state of humankind is one in which harmony is continually threatened by discord.

The story also tells us something about utopias. The perfect paradise has no people in it: people tend to spoil it. In any case, peopled or not, paradise has to be *imagined*. This gives us a first broad category of utopia: the private imagined paradise which other people cannot spoil, either because they are actually absent or else because they are ignored.

The paradises of the past were commonly of this kind. In the Golden Age, for example, where nature itself was imaginatively transformed, human harmony was simply taken for granted, whilst in the Land of Cockaigne the emphasis was placed so exclusively on personal gratification that there was neither room for nor need of other people except those catering for your desires.

RIGHT: This map of the world from the Bible of Turin may be as early as the 10th century. It is oriented in the same way as the map reproduced on page 106, with east positioned at the top.

ABOVE: A plan of the island of Utopia from the 1518 edition of Thomas More's Utopia. The first edition was published in 1516.

voice was thin, as voices from the grave." The result is that each man becomes self-centered in the truest sense, for it is now round him alone that the world slowly and gratifyingly revolves.

The Lotos-Eaters exemplify the self-indulgent dreamers who occupy a personal paradise for what in practice are fairly limited periods of drug-induced bliss. Aldous Huxley extolled the benefits of mescalin in *The Doors of Perception* (1954). Believing that these doors had been gradually closed by human evolution, Huxley, like William Blake before him, wanted to open them again. Accordingly he recommended mescalin (along with lysergic acid) as drugs of unique distinction whose use would be sure to result in valuable visionary experiences. But although like William Blake he conceived such use (which would now be called *abuse*) as a cleansing and healing process aimed at opening the doors of perception to an awareness of the true reality, few are likely to accept his theory that dependency on these mind-bending drugs is something not only acceptable but inevitable.

PRESENT AND PRIVATE

Probably the most common of all utopias is the one that accompanies a private dream. Very exceptionally this is associated with a kind of self-forgetfulness, arising from a clear-eyed recognition that true contentment is to be found by shedding all ordinary human anxieties and concerns. This is a state that Buddhists consciously and systematically set out to achieve—but they have never claimed that it is easy.

More commonly met are people whom John Carey, in his excellent collection, *A Faber Book of Utopias* (1998), calls "Robinson Crusoes of the mind," solitary utopians who see themselves inhabiting islands of their own invention. These are individuals of the sort pictured by Tennyson in his "Lotos-Eaters" (1832), seeking relief from the relentlessly oppressive Victorian values of duty and social responsibility, and finding it in an enchanted island in which every member of Odysseus's homegoing crew consumes his own portion of the delicious fruit and then, "if his fellow spake, his

Fishy Paradise

*R*upert Brooke's poem "Heaven" is a savage satire on humanity's habit of fashioning a God after its own image and picturing a paradise to match. This is how the fishes' utopian vision concludes:

> *We darkly know, by Faith we cry,*
> *The future is not Wholly Dry.*
> *Mud unto mud!—Death eddies near—*
> *Not there the appointed End, not here!*
> *But somewhere, beyond Space and Time,*
> *Is wetter water, slimier slime!*
> *And there (they trust) there swimmeth One*
> *Who swam ere rivers were begun,*
> *Immense, of fishy form and mind,*
> *Squamous, omnipotent, and kind;*
> *And under that Almighty Fin*
> *The littlest fish may enter in.*
> *Oh! never fly conceals a hook,*
> *Fish say, in the Eternal Brook,*
> *But more than mundane weeds are there,*
> *And mud, celestially fair;*
> *Fat caterpillars drift around,*
> *And Paradisal grubs are found;*
> *Unfading moths, immortal flies,*
> *And the worm that never dies.*
> *And in that Heaven of all their wish,*
> *There shall be no more land, say fish.*

We are reminded of the vision in Revelation (22:1) that "there was no more sea," and of "the worm that never dies" in the hell prophesied by Jesus (Mark 9:48).

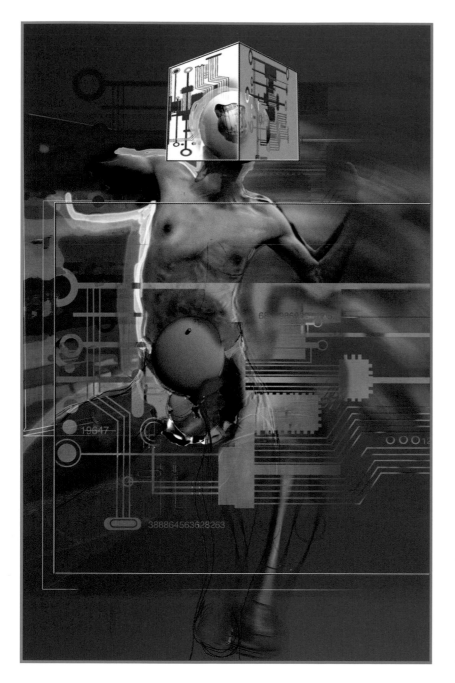

ABOVE: *Once the human body has been modified by decades of genetic engineering, it may (who knows?) come to look quite like this imaginary robot.*

FUTURE IN SPACE

In 1972 the English physicist Freeman J. Dyson gave a lecture outlining the conditions of possibility of the colonization of space. Although it reads like science fiction it was intended as a serious forecast about the future of mankind.

The lecture was given to celebrate the work of an earlier utopian, the Irishman J. D. Bernal, who had died the previous year. In 1929, long before the start of the space race, Bernal had published a book predicting that the true future of humanity lies above and beyond the planet Earth. The space pioneers, like the inhabitants of most other utopias, would be constituted quite differently from real people ("transformed" was Bernal's word).

Although Dyson comments briefly on the genetic possibilities arising from the recent discovery of the structure of DNA, he is not really interested in that aspect of Bernal's work: his own imagination was stimulated by what he called "biological engineering" and "self-reproducing machinery"; and after explaining some of the advantages these innovations would bring, he went on to point out that there are millions of comets in space amply supplied with water, carbon, and nitrogen, the basic constituents of living cells. Two things only are missing, warmth and air. "And now biological engineering will come to our rescue. We shall learn to grow trees on comets."

The lecture concludes with a prophecy that the solar system will eventually be divided into two domains. In the outer and more interesting of the two "lie the comets where trees and men will live in smaller communities, isolated from each other by huge distances. Here men will find once again the wilderness that they have lost on earth. Groups of people will be free to live as they please, independent of government authorities. Outside and away from the sun, they will be able to wander for ever on the open frontier that this planet no longer possesses."

Not, evidently, a picture that completely ignores the human race, but one bleak enough to suggest that its author has paid little attention to the effect upon society of human fears and wishes.

PUBLIC UTOPIAS

Some utopians, then—dreamers, drug addicts, and optimistic scientists—manage to evade the awkward problems faced by the rest. If you are going to dismiss or ignore the hardest problem of all, the one posed by people, you must first either be safely cocooned in drugs or dreams or else screened by scientific blinkers.

Real human beings differ. All known societies include in their number some who are sick or disabled and others, criminals or misfits, who flout the laws or conventions accepted by everybody else. So the utopian has to find some way to deal with people who for one reason or another threaten the complacency of the rest: the undesirables.

Most utopians adopt the simplest of all solutions: they get rid of the undesirables altogether. Accordingly one way of categorizing different kinds of utopias is to ask what class of people they would exclude from their ideal society: criminals, perhaps, or prostitutes, or alternatively (representing a very different conception of the origins of evil) lawyers, politicians, policemen, and bankers. We know of attempts to eliminate Jews, gypsies, and gays: Hitler's vision for Germany was unquestionably utopian in character; and so was Lenin's ideal Russia. Less reprehensible versions of utopia are hopes of a society without sickness, infirmity, or mental disability, or of one without hunger or homelessness. A list of types regarded as undesirable by various visionaries would have to include land-owners, fox-hunters, tobacco-smokers, socialists, motorists, meat-eaters, and men (Charlotte Perkins Gilman omits men altogether from her utopian *Herland* (1915)).

ELSEWHERE IN THE PAST

The writer D. H. Lawrence (1885–1930) did actually plan to realize his utopia as a genuine paradise on earth (it was to be called Rananim). Lawrence's paradise, of course, was to be very different from the Garden of Eden. It had to satisfy his own concept of the ideal human society: above all his key-value of "the inside life-throb."

Lawrence was forced to abandon this plan. Depending as it did upon the cooperation of 20 or so like-minded companions, it soon foundered on the rock that sinks all public utopias: real people. Instead Lawrence began hoping to find a real society that already matched his ideal requirements, and embarked on a series of journeys in pursuit of his elusive goal, first

BELOW: The Nuremburg rally of 1938 appeared to realize Hitler's utopian dream of a nation of mindless, super-fit, disciplined Aryan warriors.

to Sicily, then to Sri Lanka, then to Australia, to the South Sea Islands, and eventually to America, which he hated. The first Americans he met failed to meet his exacting standards, and he moved down to New Mexico. But here too the town he settled in, Taos, proved a disappointment; so in desperation he turned to the past, the vanished society of ancient Etruria. Here at last he found the phallic consciousness he had been seeking.

In *Etruscan Places* (1932) Lawrence expressed his approval of what he considered to be the two great symbols of Etruscan culture: the big phallic stones surmounting the tumuli, and the carved stone houses that stood by the doorways of certain tombs, and which suggested to him a woman's womb. It was the Etruscans' insistence on these two central symbols, the phallus and the womb, that led to their destruction. The new world, the Roman world, would have nothing to do with them: "so the whole consciousness, the whole Etruscan pulse and rhythm, must be wiped out."

One feature of Etruscan life that bothered Lawrence not a whit was the institution of slavery: the slaves, he asserts, were "by no means downtrodden menials, let the later Romans say what they will." Here is part of his description of the paintings in the tombs of Tarquinia:

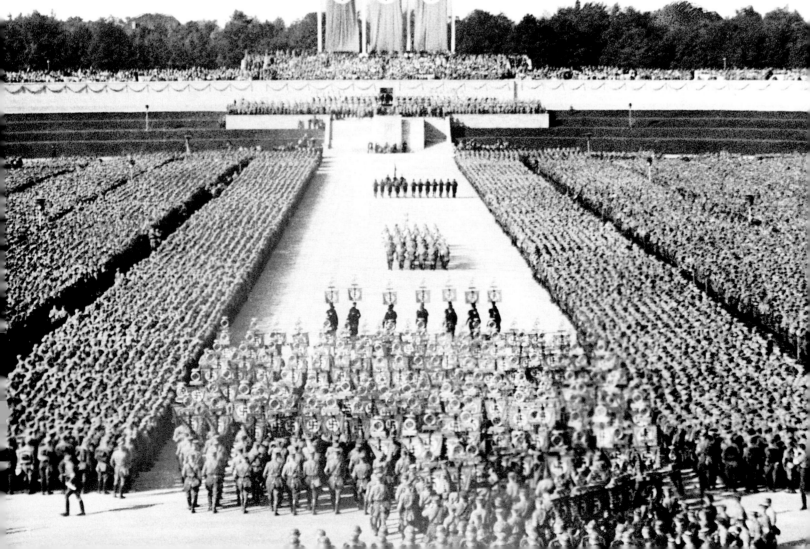

"The naked slaves joyfully stoop to the wine-jars. Their nakedness is its own clothing, more easy than drapery. The curves of their limbs show pure pleasure in life, a pleasure that goes deeper still in the limbs of the dancers, in the big, long hands thrown out and dancing to the very ends of the fingers, a dance that surges from within, like a current in the sea. It is as if the current of some strong different life swept through them, different from our shallow current today; as if they drew their vitality from different depths that we are denied."

ELSEWHERE IN THE PRESENT

Another person who literally crossed the ocean in search of paradise was the anthropologist Margaret Mead (1901–78). *Coming of Age in Samoa* (1929), her account of the nine months she spent in Samoa as a young woman in 1925–6, provoked feelings of wonder, envy, and wistful longing among her many admirers. She described a happy, carefree society which after a relatively untraumatic conversion to Christianity had remained unencumbered by the unsmiling moralities associated with the Judaeo-Christian tradition.

Mead saw the Samoans, then, as cheerful, casual, and relaxed; enjoying one another's company in every sense. The women were obliging and the men unthreatening. But as it later turned out her account was wrong on almost every point. Samoan men were warlike and aggressive, competitive and violent. Samoan society was unusually tightly structured and hierarchical. Children were brought up with great severity and punished often. Girls were expected to remain virgins until marriage; yet many proved delinquent. Mead stated that rape was virtually unknown. In fact it was twice as frequent in Samoa as in the USA.

The explanation? Simply that the friendly Samoan girls among whom Mead lived whilst in Samoa were too embarrassed to respond truthfully to her intrusive questioning. So they wove a tissue of lies ("We just fibbed and fibbed")—on which her picture of an ideal society was based.

ELSEWHERE IN THE FUTURE

Once you have identified and isolated the undesirables in your utopian society your next task is to decide what to do with them. For private utopians this is easy enough: you simply wish them away. (In Aldous Huxley's *Island* (1962) two pink pills swallowed after meals were enough to cure people of antisocial

---

Settling For Less

*I*n his poem "Report from Paradise" Zbigniew Herbert settles for less:

In paradise the work week is fixed at thirty hours
salaries are higher prices steadily go down
manual labor is not tiring
(because of reduced gravity)
chopping wood is no harder than typing
the social system is stable and the rulers are wise
really in paradise one is better off than
in whatever country

At first it was to have been different
luminous circles choirs and degrees of abstraction
but they were not able to separate exactly
the soul from the flesh and so it would come here
with a drop of fat a thread of muscle
it was necessary to face the consequences
to mix a grain of the absolute with a grain of clay
one more departure from doctrine the last departure
only John foresaw it: you will be resurrected
in the flesh

not many behold God
he is only for those of 100 per cent pneuma
the rest listen to communiqués about miracles
and floods
some day God will be seen by all
when it will happen nobody knows

As it is now every Saturday at noon
sirens sweetly bellow
and from the factories go the heavenly proletarians
awkwardly under their arms they carry their wings
like violins

Shangri-La

*A*t the Lost Horizon of James Hilton's 1933 novel of that name, paradise and utopia blend indistinguishably together, for the Buddhist monastery of Shangri-La in the Tibetan hills toward which the characters of the novel laboriously make their way is situated in the inscrutable East, which is where Christian writers and explorers had located the lost paradise of Eden.

Once Hilton's travelers have arrived at their destination the pages describing the mountain paradise are as evocative as anything in earlier literature. "It was, indeed, a strange and almost incredible sight. A group of colored pavilions clung to the mountainside with none of the grim deliberation of a Rhineland castle, but rather with the chance delicacy of flower-petals impaled upon a crag."

Shangri-La provides all that any cultivated westerner could possibly desire in the way of climate, food, accommodation, entertainment, and even (though this is deliberately understated) sex. All these delights are accompanied by a remarkable promise, not of immortality (which is not on offer) but of exceptional longevity and enduring health and vitality. Unusually, then, the inhabitants of Shangri-La have all the time they need for relaxation, contemplation, learning, and repose. There is only one snag: they are prisoners, and will never be allowed to return home.

tendencies.) But when, as is usually the case, your projected utopia is going to be occupied by real people, there is more of a problem.

Broadly speaking there are two classes of undesirable, the criminal and the sick (Samuel Butler's *Erewhon* (1872) effectively reverses these two categories, treating sick people as criminals and criminals as sick, but this is a *dystopia*). At present the possibility of reforming criminals or of eliminating disease altogether seems remote (utopian!), but no doubt certain methods of genetic tampering that are currently being tested will, once available, be applied. As soon as this happens they will be taken down from the high shelf of utopian dreams and placed alongside other preventative medicines used in inoculations and immunizations that were once out of reach on the same shelf. But nobody has yet forecast the imminent prevention of *all* disease, and few are likely to welcome unreservedly H. G. Wells' remark concerning "the merciful obliteration of weak and silly and pointless things." (*Anticipations*, 1901)

In principle the eradication of disease is clearly something to be welcomed. But what about criminals and social misfits? Some of the various methods (such as castration and lobotomy) used to prevent people from committing crimes of violence may seem too drastic. Perhaps the method most likely to win the applause of utopians is behavioral engineering, and in fact this was seriously proposed as an engine of social control by the American psychologist B. F. Skinner (1904–90), whose utopian novel, *Walden Two* (1948), caused a furor.

Skinner had himself succeeded in altering the behavioral patterns of many animals by the careful adjustment of chosen stimuli over a period of time. He was of the opinion that certain undesirable features of human behavior too could be modified by systematic training. Frazier, the founder of the commune portrayed in his novel, had managed to rid its members of emotions such as fear, hate, and rage; and since he believed that one of the causes of these was natural human competitiveness he got rid of that too.

Skinner was accused by some of flying in the face of human freedom. He argued, however, that *all* human action, both before and after the application of psychological conditioning, can be seen as simply a response to certain stimuli. In any case, one might wish to call into question, as Anthony Burgess did in *A Clockwork Orange* (1962), the very aim of somehow eliminating even the most violent of the antisocial tendencies of people like Burgess' protagonist, the lawless Alex. The aversion therapy for which Alex

volunteers in prison turns him into a couch potato. Like many other utopias, Skinner's ideal commune could easily be transformed into a dystopia.

CANDIDE

Early on in Voltaire's satirical tale, *Candide* (1759), its eponymous hero is caught embracing the beautiful daughter of the owner of the country home in Westphalia where he resides, and is expelled from this earthly paradise. A series of adventures all over the globe convinces him that his traveling-companion, the family tutor Dr Pangloss, is wrong to hold that this is the best of all possible worlds. Candide ends up, famously, by reflecting that: "We must tend our garden." What we have on earth is no paradise, but a garden all the same, and it is up to us to look after it. Another well-known phrase of Voltaire is surely the wisest thing ever said on the subject of utopias: we should be ready to settle for something less than perfection because "the best is the enemy of the good."

BELOW: Illustration from Voltaire's Candide, *written in 1759. Candide, accompanied by his trusty servant Cacambo, visits Surinam, in South America. A black slave who has had a leg and a hand cut off while working in a sugar factory tells them: "This is the price of eating sugar in Europe."*

CLOSE TO
NATURE

IN THE MAJOR MONOTHEISTIC FAITHS, THE DIVINE OFTEN STANDS APART FROM NATURE AND HAS CONTROL OVER IT; NATURE IS GOD'S DOMINION. YET IN OTHER RELIGIONS, THE IDEA OF NATURE IS OFTEN SYNONYMOUS WITH THE CONCEPT OF THE DIVINE: THE EARTH IS SACRED, A SOURCE OF LIFE, AND ALL LIFE ULTIMATELY RETURNS TO NATURE.

Chapter

10

This chapter explores a range of religious movements in which Nature is seen as a manifestation of the sacred. Biblical ideas of paradise and heaven strongly influence Rastafarianism and Shembe's Nazareth Church, but emphasize the importance of this world rather than the next. For Aboriginal Australians, Nature resonates with the power of the Dreamtime. In America, the natural landscape that has long been regarded as a potential Eden is often introduced into Native American religions as the setting of the "Happy Hunting Ground."

LEFT: Ayers Rock in the Northern Territory, Australia is an important Aboriginal site. Aborigines believe it to have risen miraculously from a sandhill in the creation period of the Dreamtime.

BELOW: The religious rituals of the Aborigines focus on the epic deeds of creator ancestors and supernatural beings, enabling them to experience the power of the Dreamtime and maintain a harmonious relationship with nature.

AUSTRALIAN ABORIGINES IDENTIFY CLOSELY WITH THEIR ENVIRONMENT, BELIEVING THAT NATURE IS A CREATIVE FORCE. ALL OBJECTS AND LIVING BEINGS IN NATURE POSSESS THE SAME ETERNAL AND ANIMATING SPIRIT, THE DREAMING (OR DREAMTIME). ABORIGINAL MYTHS FOCUS UPON THE ANCESTRAL BEINGS OF THE CREATION PERIOD. THIS IS QUITE DIFFERENT FROM ANY WESTERN UNDERSTANDING OF PARADISE: ABORIGINAL MYTHS DO NOT FOCUS ON AN ENCLOSED GARDEN; NOR DO THEY LOOK BACK TO A LOST GOLDEN AGE, A PERIOD OF BLISS THAT IS NOW OUT OF REACH OF MORTALS.

AUSTRALIAN ABORIGINES

THE DREAMING

The Dreaming refers to a time beyond living memory, when creator ancestors and supernatural beings traveled across a featureless world. Through their actions, both moral and immoral, these beings shaped the world into the form in which it now appears and helped establish the spiritual and moral order that influences Aboriginal life. The ancestors then disappeared, died, became part of the earth and features of the terrain, or returned to the sky from which they had come.

The Dreaming is still sacred and still apparent in the present. Whatever the fate of the ancestral heroes, an aura of immortality remains; their power is within each individual and can become apparent in religious ritual, influencing the affairs of men and women. While the Dreamtime refers to an ancient age, this age is not lost. It is ever-present and can be accessed through ritual, dreams, and physical journeys.

THE LAND OF THE DEAD

A common theme in Aboriginal belief is that the human spirit leaves the human body in death and exists in a ghostlike form, journeying to a new life in the land of the dead, where it joins the ancestors who traveled there in the Dreaming. Often the land of the dead is described as the "sky country," although sometimes it is understood to be a mythical island "beyond the greater water" or in "the northern ocean"; alternatively, it might be called "the cloudland" or "beyond the clouds" or simply situated "to the west." This is not a place of punishment or reward: people's behavior on this earth does not influence their afterlife. The land of the dead is an idyllic place which is similar to the earth, except it is more fertile, water is plentiful and there is an abundance of game. Life for the spirit is therefore similar to life as it was on earth, but easier.

Although the spirit no longer lives on earth, it is not totally detached from human life. Burial customs are an important part of Aboriginal culture and they show how the living expect the deceased to have influence in the human world. In the customs, the living pay respect to the deceased, but they also encourage the spirit on its journey in an attempt to prevent it from lingering in this world, or exercising any malignant influence if it becomes trapped and unable to continue on its way.

Yet even after having successfully journeyed to the land of the dead, the spirit can return, visiting the earth from the sky. Back in this world, it might linger in its earthly "haunts" or wander about the bush, eating the remains of meals and enjoying deserted camp fires. The living may also encounter spirits in their waking dreams, and Aboriginal doctors are able to visit the land of the dead to receive advice and knowledge.

The journey made by the spirit to reach the land of the dead is an important part of Aboriginal belief. The spirit follows the route taken by the ancestral beings in their mythical journey. Like them, the spirit might ascend on the rays of the setting sun or by climbing a rope lowered down from the sky country by the ancestral beings. Alternatively, the spirit might have to cross an invisible bridge or reach the sky by journeying along the Milky Way.

During the journey, supernatural beings test the spirit. For the Gunwiggu Aborigines of western Arnhem land, the spirit might have his front teeth knocked out: if the gums bleed, the spirit is sent back to the body; if they do not bleed, then it is certain that the spirit has left the body for good, and is allowed to continue its journey to the land of the dead.

A RETURN TO THE DREAMING

Some Aborigines believe that the spirit merges with the ancestral beings that are already in the land of the dead, rather than joining them as an individual. Alternatively, the deceased may have more than one spirit; one might travel to the land of the dead, whilst another remains on earth.

Many Central Australian tribes do not hope for a future life in a land of the dead at all. There is a land of the dead, but it is the home of the gods, not humans. According to the western Aranda, the sky gods visited the earth during the dreamtime and subsequently returned to the sky. Their sky home is eternally green and they live on fruits and vegetables, which are

plentiful. The Milky Way flows through the land like a broad river, so there is no drought; the other stars are their campfires.

The western Aranda do not believe that humans will ever journey to the land of the dead. Instead, the spirit of the deceased inevitably becomes a part of the Dreaming, the essential power of the universe. The essence of a person thus continues after death not by becoming a ghost but by merging with its source and being a part of this power until it is eventually reborn on earth, as a human or animal or even as a stone—it does not matter which, for all things contain the power of the Dreaming. From this perspective, death itself is a form of birth: it is entry to the Dreaming.

BELOW: A modern Aboriginal bark painting of a funeral ceremony with kangaroo on Croker Island, painted by Melangi de Milingibi. Funeral ceremonies center upon the journey of the deceased's soul.

Most African religions do not express the notion of a blessed afterlife in the hereafter. Occasionally, for example among the Bachwa in the Congo, it is thought that the next life will involve no illness, hunger, or death, but will contain happiness, comfort, and easy hunting instead. Most religions advocate belief in an ancestral afterlife in which the recently deceased exist as spirits on this earth and are still intimately involved in the activities of the family.

AFRICAN RELIGIONS

RIGHT: A crown from the Yoruba people of Nigeria worn by an oba (local chief) at festivals and sacred occasions. The bead veiling prevents the oba from being seen directly, which suggests to onlookers that he is a divine presence and situated, at least partly, in the spirit world.

This brief exploration of African religions therefore focuses on the concept of paradise within creation stories—though even here one has to be cautious about applying the word, since "paradise" is not an important concept within African religions. The "here and now" is the focus of religious activity and members of African religions do not tend to distinguish between the sacred and the secular, the visible and the invisible world. Nor is it easy to separate the concepts of "myth" and "history," both of which are closely interwoven with the priorities of daily living. A kind of paradise can be identified within the creation stories, but this paradise is usually incidental to the stories rather than the central focus.

CREATION STORIES

One of the stories commonly found in different African cultures focuses on the relationship between man and God and tells how, far in man's past, the earth and sky became separated. These stories are similar to that of the Fall in the Book of Genesis, although their function within society is very different from the role the Bible story has had within Christianity.

One story, versions of which are told throughout Africa, focuses on the relationship between man and God, earth and sky: originally, people lived on the sky and were immortal. One day they cut holes in the floor of the sky and lowered down ropes which reached all the way to earth. Each day people would climb down the ropes to visit the earth. Some of the people were mischievous (in different versions, the mischief might be caused by animals rather than people) and the creator God had these pranksters guarded in the sky so that they would not cause trouble. One day, however, the tricksters evaded the guards, escaped down to earth, and cut the ropes, forever separating

the earth from the sky. The rope may symbolize immortality, for when the rope was cut, the route to immortality was severed.

In these stories, the stars are often regarded as holes in the sky, through which the ropes were lowered. There are many exceptions, for example within South African Zulu accounts, the stars were once animals, or the eyes of the departed looking down at the world. The stories are as much about the reason why there are stars as they are about the relationship between earth and sky.

Amongst the Tutsi cattle herders of Rwanda, the divine realm of the sky was believed to be prosperous and beautiful. The supreme being for the Tutsis, the god Imana, created all things in the sky and man enjoyed a harmonious relationship with nature. In the divine realm there was no need to work, since the trees and fields provided plenty of produce. Even hunting was easy, for animals were not afraid of man and therefore did not run away. There was no sickness, and if for any reason someone ever did die, Imana would bring them back to life again after a short period; yet this too, was a paradise now lost.

Different stories of the distant past provide different details. Sometimes it is the cattle that are wonderfully sleek and fat, but a drought might force an unsuccessful move to fresh pastures; or people might become impatient and set out in search of a wonderful new land of their own without success.

Most of these tales are consistent in that they picture a world in which man was originally close to God and to nature, but became separated from them. However, these stories are not centrally concerned with paradise; their emphasis on the origins of mankind and a severed relationship with a divine creator are intended to explain the realities of living in the present world, and the importance of social structure. They operate on clear lines of opposites: order versus chaos, peace versus conflict, mediocrity versus perfection—but the extent to which there is a "paradise lost" is seldom the point of the story. They tell how the world is subject to change and renewal, and justify the need of rules for social living and ritual action which will overcome any distance between the human and the divine.

The clearest African concepts of paradise, are to be found not among the indigenous African religions, but in the African Christian movements. These have a much stronger deliberate emphasis on paradise and heaven. A fine example of this is the Nazareth Church in South Africa, founded by the Zulu prophet Isiah Shembe.

ABOVE: A funeral ceremony in Ghana. Red shoulder wraps indicate a direct relationship with the deceased. Death leads to the spirit world, from where the deceased protect their descendants, remaining intimately involved in the events of this world.

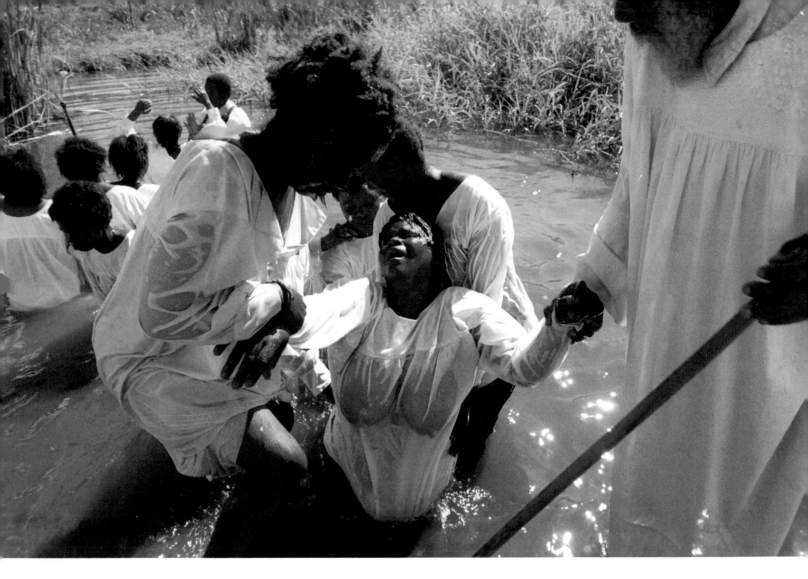

THE NAZARETH CHURCH

Isiah Shembe's church is not the largest of the so-called African Independent Churches (movements which merge African and Christian rituals, or which have broken away from their missionary founders) but it is one of the best known.

Isiah Shembe was born around 1870. He became a preacher, prophet and healer—able to cast out spirits—in 1911, after illness and a series of visions. Formerly a Baptist, he founded the Nazareth Church. Working as a laborer, he traveled around the Natal area of South Africa, healing, preaching, and casting out spirits. He preached barefoot and left his hair uncut. He taught the importance of the Ten Commandments, as well as many Old Testament laws, stressing the commandment that one must not work on the sabbath, and the rule that forbade the eating of pork; smoking and the drinking of alcohol are also banned among his followers.

In 1913, Isiah Shembe bought land for a church a short distance from Durban. He built the church on a wooded hillock at a place called Ekuphakameni. In Zulu this means "high place" but since Shembe was buried in a small mausoleum there in 1935 his followers have called it "paradise" or "heaven on earth." Instead of regarding Shembe as a prophet, they often see him as a messiah, standing alongside Jesus in significance, or even replacing him as the Christ of the Zulus.

Shembe created a religious and social order that greatly values the sacred sites he established. These sites have given a new meaning to the idea of land for the typically poor congregants who often own none and for them Ekuphakameni is land of special significance.

Church members are able to gain salvation at Ekuphakameni. Each year, thousands of church members gather for the July festival and travel to the sacred hill—there are often up to 100,000 followers, all visiting "paradise." They find the holy village of Ekuphakameni surrounded by an enclosure. They have to enter through gates which are regarded as the gates of heaven, guarded by ancestral spirits. The congregation believes that the spirits of the ancestors act as angels, keeping out sinners but allowing the righteous to pass into the village (which they refer to as a city).

In the hymns of the church, the village of Ekuphakemeni is often identified as a garden and as the Garden of Eden, but the real paradise lies at the heart of the village, where Shembe's congregants gather in their white robes for a service in which they drink from the "water of life." They regain paradise in this exalted place, establishing (or re-establishing) lives of purity.

The idea that Ekuphakameni is paradise is not a sentiment that is likely to be shared by Christians who belong to churches other than Shembe's. Conceptually, the idea is also a departure from the traditional tenets of western Christianity. The established western churches often stress the otherworldly aspects of paradise and heaven and, whereas there have been attempts to build Jerusalems on this earth, these churches generally look back to a paradise lost and forward to a paradise that can be regained. The latter is therefore the setting for events that may not even take place on this earth. In contrast, Shembe's Ekuphakameni firmly brings the idea of salvation back from the "otherworld" to the present; this is broadly consistent with the indigenous African religious views we have explored on pages 142-143 and is an important example of how Shembe's church has molded established patterns of Christian thinking into an African framework. For Shembe's followers, paradise is an imminent event, which can be experienced by all. Eden can be re-created by the believer and re-found; Ekuphakameni is pivotal in this experience.

Important ideas about the role of paradise in Shembe's own thinking can clearly be seen in the hymns which Shembe composed and which are sung at Ekuphakameni in rituals of dance and drummed music:

> Come ye all,
> Let us go to Ekuphakameni
> We shall be richly anointed
> with an ointment of grace.

In other words, the paradise of Ekuphakameni provides salvation. It heals the spirit. In another of Shembe's hymns, we see Shembe addressing the Creator God, expressing the viewpoint that without God's healing (his "ointment of grace"), Shembe will remain lost, in a similar situation to Adam after the Fall in Genesis:

> You placed me in that Garden
> For thy great love's sake…
> I am in need, my Lord,
> of soap to wash me
> Return me in haste
> to the bliss that was mine.

The Fall has separated humans from God but, according to Shembe, God is the "God of Adam," by which he means "the God of all men," and salvation is available to all at Ekuphakameni. The common Christian idea of heaven as being another realm "up there" is neglected but not rejected; "up there" is simply not the focus of concern for the congregation. It is important to add that Ekuphakameni is not only associated with paradise—the church also links it to the City of Jerusalem and with Bethlehem, the place of Jesus' birth. Within the beliefs of Shembe's followers, it is as if Ekuphakameni lies at the heart of God's creation, as though the paradaisaic church on the hill is both fulfillment and expression of all biblical history and belief.

BELOW: A member of the Nazareth Church wears photographs of church leaders. Isiah Shembe is pictured on the far right.

RASTAFARIANISM IS A MESSIANIC MOVEMENT BASED IN JAMAICA AND MADE FAMOUS BY THE REGGAE MUSIC OF THE SINGER BOB MARLEY. RASTAFARIANS ARE CONCERNED WITH ISSUES OF INEQUALITY, OPPRESSION, AND SLAVERY; THE MOVEMENT EMERGED IN THE 1920S AND THEIR POLITICAL IDEAS DEVELOPED BROADLY IN PARALLEL WITH THE AMERICAN CIVIL RIGHTS MOVEMENT.

RASTAFARIAN PARADISE

Most Rastafarians are ex-Christians and the Bible is central to their beliefs. Although they have no established churches or religious leaders, Rastafarians often meet in small informal groups to discuss the truths contained within biblical text. They often use ganja (cannabis) to assist their reflections upon the scriptures and to help find God's message.

Ganja is an essential part of the religious practice. As the "holy herb" it assists the Rastafarians in their search for meaning and revealed truth, enabling them to enjoy what they regard as a direct experience of God. Smoking ganja is therefore an act of affirmation and of faith. Their use of the drug is grounded in their understanding of various biblical passages, such as the Genesis creation story: "and the earth brought forth grass, and herb bearing seed after his kind ... and God saw that it was good." In addition, the use of ganja serves as a protest against the status quo and the dominant global political order which they believe has denied them access to their African roots.

Within the process of meditating on the truth, the Bible is an invaluable source of inspiration. For Rastafarians, God's message is closely linked to the theme of liberation. They have read the Old Testament concerns about exile, slavery, and the promised land (which originally applied to the Israelites), as well as the prophecies in the New Testament's Book of Revelation regarding the overthrow of the existing order or "Babylon" (which originally applied to Rome) and adapted these concepts to their own modern Jamaican situation. They believe that they too are exiled as a result of slavery, but that salvation is possible and will come through spiritual identification with (or repatriation to) Africa.

These beliefs of exile and homecoming are closely linked to Rastafarian beliefs in paradise and heaven: Jamaica will always be a foreign land, its occupation the result of slavery rather than of God's divine plan, whereas Africa—and especially Ethiopia—is home. For Rastafarians, Ethiopia is the origin of all culture,

RIGHT: Bob Marley's lyrics communicated the Rastafarian message to the world, stressing the importance of natural living and the expectation of a spiritual homecoming to the promised land of Africa.

OPPOSITE: Rastafarians proclaim the late Haile Selassie, former Emperor of Ethiopia, to be the divine messiah who will return his people from slavery.

the original Eden and the abode of God; as such, it is both paradise and heaven. Rastafarianism rejects the idea of the otherworld: God does not belong in the sky, he belongs on earth in the promised land of Ethiopia.

THE AFRICAN HOMELAND

The importance of Ethiopia lies in biblical references to it, in the fact that it is the only African country never to have been officially colonized, and also in the impressive coronation of Emperor Haile Selassie to the Ethiopian throne in 1930. Haile Selassie ("Lord of Lords and King of Kings of Ethiopia, Conquering Lion of the Tribe of Judah, the Elect of God, and the Light of the World") is a manifestation of the living God, despite his earthly death and burial. He is the Black Messiah who will return his people to the homeland of Africa. His name before he became Emperor was Ras Tafari (it should be remembered that while Haile Selassie is the focus of the movement, he did not help found or join it; he was a devout Christian).

Many Rastafarians are aware that Ethiopia is economically impoverished, ravaged by the effects of war; but this, they believe, will all change: they will help restore Ethiopia to its rightful state when they return to develop their Eden. They will create a new society, in an eternal age of plenty and of freedom, after an apocalyptic day of judgment which will destroy Babylon and usher in justice, peace, and prosperity.

The relationship Rastafarians have with nature is central to the establishing of a new Eden. God is so closely identified with nature that many Rastafarians have stated that the two are one and the same. They believe that humans must observe the rules of nature in order to live well and harmoniously, and that nature does not just exist in the world, but also exists within the individual, as a creative force. By harnessing this force, and living in harmony with nature, Rastafarians believe that they will eventually be able to re-create Eden and re-discover what was lost. To do so, they leave the earth in peace, for the earth is the Lord's.

Rastafarians reject the use of processed foods and synthetic fertilizers; they do not eat tinned produce, or any food unless they know its origins. Milk, coffee, soft drinks, and alcohol are regarded as unnatural, the use of preservatives is banned, and food is cooked as lightly as possible.

In their use of ganja, their strong emphasis on self-employment, and even in their diet they affirm their belief that the existing political order is evil—it is Babylon (the biblical city of sin). Thus Rastafarians attempt to challenge the dominant economic, social, and political world order through the ways in which they engage with it.

ONE OF THE COMMON ASSUMPTIONS ABOUT NATIVE AMERICAN CONCEPTS OF THE AFTERLIFE IS THAT THERE IS A WIDESPREAD BELIEF IN AN IDYLLIC SPIRIT EXISTENCE, A "HAPPY HUNTING GROUND," A PHRASE MADE FAMOUS BY THE NOVELIST JAMES FENIMORE COOPER IN *THE LAST OF THE MOHICANS* (1826). IN A BOOK ABOUT PARADISE, SUCH A TOPIC CAN HARDLY BE IGNORED, BUT IT SHOULD BE NOTED AT THE OUTSET THAT THE NUMBER OF PEOPLE WHO THINK THAT THE NATIVE AMERICANS BELIEVED IN A HAPPY HUNTING GROUND IS FAR GREATER THAN THE NUMBER OF THOSE WHO ACTUALLY DID. THE PURPOSE OF THIS BRIEF EXPLORATION OF THE HAPPY HUNTING GROUND IS TO SHOW HOW NATIVE AMERICAN AFTERLIFE IDEAS HAVE HISTORICALLY BEEN PORTRAYED, RATHER THAN TO ASSESS THE VALIDITY OF THE PORTRAYALS.

THE AMERICAN EDEN

THE HAPPY HUNTING GROUND

To put the discussion in context: while most American Indian cultures believe that the spirit or soul of a person is immortal, conceptions of the afterlife are often vague. Different tribes have different beliefs which range from the very optimistic to the idea that the afterlife can be only a pale shadow of the life enjoyed on earth. Despite this variation, there is a general agreement amongst Native American religions that responsibility lies in living harmoniously with the natural and moral order of this life, rather than in working toward supernatural salvation in the next.

Christian missionaries were the first people to report on the belief in the Happy Hunting Ground, and their reports are colored by their own proselytizing agenda. As a result, these records have to be treated with some suspicion.

As the wording of "Happy Hunting Ground" suggests, the Native American afterlife is supposedly a heavenly place, where the souls of the dead will find hunting easy and enjoy an abundance of all the things that made their earthly lives pleasant. One of the earliest written accounts of Native American beliefs was provided by the Jesuit Father Joseph Jouvency in 1610:

They believe that that appointed place for souls, to which after death they are to retire, is in the direction of the setting sun, and there they are to enjoy feasting, hunting, and dancing.

In 1634, Father Paul Le Jeune reported on the beliefs of the Montagnais Indians, stating that the souls of the dead are immortal and "go very far away to a large village situated where the sun sets." His report was less optimistic than Jouvency's. According to Le Jeune, the soul is the shadow of the man, a dark and sombre image. The dead have an existence similar to that of the living, except that in the afterlife certain rules are reversed:

Souls are not like us, they do not see at all during the day, and see very clearly at night, their day is in the darkness of the night, and their night in the light of the day.

Souls live at night and rest by day. The seasons are reversed and the soul walks cross-legged. When Le Jeune asked what the souls of the dead hunted, the response suggested that the world of the dead is a soul-world and that all things have souls. He wrote:

They hunt for the souls of beavers, porcupines, moose, and other animals, using the soul of the snow-shoes to walk upon the soul of the snow, which is in yonder country; in short, they make use of the souls of all things, as we here use the things themselves.

Le Jeune makes no reference to beliefs that when looking up at the night sky it is possible to see the souls of the dead; however, he did stress that the Native Americans he interviewed called the Milky Way *Tchipaï meskenau* "the path of souls," since this was the route that the soul took to the village in the sky. On the journey, souls fed by eating the bark of trees.

The seventeenth-century writer Nicolas Perrot wrote extensively of the Northern Algonkian Ottawa Indians, who had sophisticated beliefs about the nature of the journey to the land of the dead. Stories of these journeys are widespread in Native American religions and are known to historians as the Orpheus tradition after the Ancient Greek myth in which Orpheus visits the underworld. Indeed Native Americans generally seem to have been more concerned with the journey to the land of the dead than with the place itself, irrespective of whether or not the ultimate destination was idyllic.

BELOW: View from Scott's Bluff, above Nebraska Prairie. The novelist James Fenimore Cooper adapted the traditions of the early missionaries and turned the American landscape into a fictitious heaven, the "Happy Hunting Ground" of Native Americans.

ABOVE: *The northern lights. Many Native Americans believed the northern lights to be the abode of the dead. Many Eskimo groups have a myth of the northern lights being the spirits of the dead playing football with the head of a walrus. The Eskimos of east Greenland believed that children who died at birth caused the northern lights by their dancing.*

"And now," observes Adam, "we must again try to discover what sort of world this is, and why we have been sent hither."
(HAWTHORNE, THE NEW ADAM AND EVE)

THE AMERICAN GENESIS

For the Founding Fathers, America was paradise, a new world ordained by God, the golden land in a golden age. They saw the future of a new nation open out like the landscape in front of them—a second Eden and the promised land, a sanctuary far removed from the decadence of the English old world society they had left behind.

The early settlers had conflicting and complex reactions to the indigenous Native American population that they encountered, understanding them at one extreme to be an evil and corrupt presence in the garden—"Black Devils"—and at the other extreme as innocent noble savages, who were as naked as Adam and Eve before the Fall and who were enjoying the fruits of plenty in an unspoiled garden. Both these patronizing perspectives seemed to them to offer proof that America, although not heaven, was heaven sent.

The emerging expansionist policies of the settling European Americans soon led to the eviction of Native Americans from the new Eden. Yet the violence with which this was done did not put an end to the myth that America was a paradise, a myth that has continued to affect the nation's sense of identity and destiny, to influence its writers and inform their understanding of nature.

NATURE AND THE LITERARY LANDSCAPE

Native Americans in general hold complicated views of Nature, believing it to be a manifestation of a divine and supernatural power which is present in all living creatures and all things. Yet a simplistic European American understanding of these beliefs, coupled with continuing expansionism, were strong influences in the developing metaphors of the frontier hero and the backwoodsman. The fighter at the harsh frontier was seen as combating the savages in order to expand the American Eden, a mission in which he would become a real man and a hero; while the backwoodsman, exchanging the clothing and equipment of civilization for hunting gear and canoe and moving from the city to live in a log cabin within Nature, would take on all the virtues of the Noble Savage.

According to Perrot, the Ottawa land of the dead was a true paradise, a beautiful and fertile land where the climate is neither cold nor hot, where there is an abundance of animals and birds, and hunters are never in danger of attack when they seek food. "As soon as the soul has left the body it enters this charming country" and continues to travel, encountering obstacles that have to be overcome, such as a rapid river that has to be crossed by a bridge made from a slim tree-trunk, which is so pliable that the unsuspecting soul might be swept away by the waters and drowned. This is especially risky for the old and the very young.

The river is full of fish, which the souls can eat to sustain themselves, and having survived the perils of the journey the soul arrives in a delightful country, full of the fruits of nature. Sweet-scented flowers cover the ground and from a short distance away comes the sound of drumming. The newly arrived soul approaches the sound, discovers other souls dancing enthusiastically, and is welcomed by them and feasted.

When they have finished eating they go to mingle with the others—to dance and make merry forever, without being any longer subject to sorrow, anxiety, or infirmities, or to any of the vicissitudes of mortal life.

Montagnais-Naskapi afterlife beliefs received new attention nearly 300 years after Le Jeune, in the writings of (amongst others) Frank Speck. His account is broadly similar to Le Jeune's missionary report, although he presents two different ideas which, if not actually contradictory, do seem to conflict. For now, instead of journeying via the Milky Way, "the souls of individuals become transformed into stars and rest in the firmament until they become reincarnated." However, somewhat at variance to this, Speck also makes clear that there is an abode of souls in the sky, which is visible in the form of stars; that the dead do travel over the Milky Way or "ghost road"; and that they meet in a dance and light up the sky as the northern lights.

The issue of how the European American could be at one with nature, and how to live in order to become noble and free, was an important concern. It preoccupied Ralph Waldo Emerson, an influential nineteenth-century American writer, who frequently stressed that all people should be lovers of Nature:

In the woods, is perpetual youth. Within these plantations of God, a purity and sanctity reign, a perennial festival is dressed, and the guest sees not how he should tire of them in a thousand years. In the woods, we return to reason and faith. ("Nature," 1836)

For Emerson, it is by embracing Nature that the individual moves toward the spiritual perfections of love and the good, for by immersing oneself in Nature one can come to understand the divine order.

Essayist and poet Henry David Thoreau, writing in the 1860s, explicitly linked the wilds of America to the Eden of the Book of Genesis:

As a true patriot, I should be ashamed to think that Adam in paradise was more favorably situated on the whole than the backwoodsman in this country. ("Walking," 1862)

Thoreau urged his readers not to squander this paradise. Indeed, one must nurture and sustain Nature, as Nature in turn "is doing her best each moment to make us well ... Nature is but another name for health" ("Huckleberries," 1861). No wonder then that he urges his readers toward Nature with this exhortation: "Let us try to keep the new world new."

The extent to which Americans have managed to do so is one of the major issues of the nation's literature and articulates an essential paradox: the desire to recover the lost innocence enjoyed in Eden and yet combine it with the wisdom brought by the Fall. The American Adam wants to be back in the garden, but clothed rather than naked, innocent yet equipped with the knowledge of good and evil.

In *East of Eden*, John Steinbeck's fictional heroes struggle with the competing values of innocence and experience, optimism and doubt, as they attempt to build a future and a destiny. Steinbeck turns the garden into a plowed field and as they work the land—or try to find land they can work—Steinbeck argues that although it is possible to remain innocent, one must still take responsibility for that innocence.

The title "East of Eden" is itself a quote from the Book of Genesis, where Adam and Eve's son Cain, a farmer ("a tiller of the ground"), kills his brother Abel out of envy. Whereas God punished Adam by forcing him to work the earth, he punishes Cain by distancing him from that land. "Cursed from the earth" (in other words, unable to farm well), Cain becomes a fugitive and vagabond, a fallen figure living "East of Eden."

In the novel, Steinbeck explores the extent to which American society shares Cain's fate: the land is both the root of America's hopes and the possible setting for its decline. Steinbeck's farming characters are both blessed and damned. The fictional character Adam has no Eden and is determined to buy one. He marries Cathy—an evil woman with an angelic face but a tongue that, snakelike, flicks around her lips—and they move to California. He builds a garden farm around her, but she shoots him, flees from it and crushes both his ambition and his dream of Eden.

In the works of F. Scott Fitzgerald, there is a feeling that the new world has already grown old. In *The Great Gatsby*, the hero Gatsby deliberately re-invents and re-creates himself. He has changed his name and turned his back on his genealogical roots in search of a new life; yet corruption lurks around his lifestyle and eventually he is murdered. F. Scott Fizgerald's point is simple but profound: the killing of Gatsby is also the killing of America, because what he wanted is what America also needs, a second chance at innocence.

In *The Diamond as Big as the Ritz*, by the same author, the owner of the diamond, Washington, stoops to trying to bribe God in an attempt to ensure that he does not fall from his position of enormous wealth. God does not accept the bribe, but even God does not escape criticism: one of the two surviving characters declares that youth (i.e. innocence) is a chemical madness and that "his was a great sin who first invented consciousness."

Put another way: according to Fitzgerald, innocence is unrealistic; and yet reflecting upon the American dream—or even just being conscious of it—will prevent the dream from becoming reality.

BELOW: *A still from the movie adaptation of* East of Eden, *in which the characters act out the possibilities and tensions of the American Dream, in pursuit of love and happiness.*

I N THE 1960S, THE SCIENTIST JAMES LOVELOCK DEVELOPED THE PROPOSITION THAT THE PLANET IS A SUPER-ORGANISM, AN INTERRELATED WHOLE, WHICH REGULATES ITS OWN SYSTEM IN A WAY THAT ALLOWS LIFE TO EXIST ON THE PLANET. THE BASIS OF HIS HYPOTHESIS LIES IN A COMPLEX ANALYSIS OF THE EARTH'S SURFACE TEMPERATURE, THE COMPONENTS OF THE ATMOSPHERE, THE LEVEL OF SALT IN THE OCEANS AND OTHER FACTORS. HE ARGUED THAT THE EARTH IS RESILIENT AND CAPABLE, IF DISTURBED BY HUMAN INTERFERENCE, OF ADJUSTING TO A NEW EQUILIBRIUM IN WHICH HUMANS WILL BE UNABLE TO SURVIVE. THE NOVELIST WILLIAM GOLDING PROVIDED LOVELOCK WITH A METAPHOR TO HELP TO EXPLAIN THIS CENTRAL IDEA, THE NAME OF THE ANCIENT GREEK EARTH MOTHER: GAIA.

BELOW: The Greek Earth Mother, Gaia, suckling her divine children in a fertile grove. Detail of a 12th-century bronze portal at the San Zeno Maggiore in Verona, Italy.

EARTH: THE GLOBAL GARDEN

Lovelock's theory caused controversy within the scientific community and (in part because of the Gaia label) was greeted with enthusiasm by many New Age followers who saw it as support of their belief that earth has a consciousness and is alive, a "she" rather than an "it."

Throughout this book we have regularly addressed the expectation that there is a new age around the corner (if it has not already arrived) and explored beliefs that humans are in essence spiritual beings. We have seen the idea expressed in many religions that to live well humankind must live harmoniously with Nature, as there is a oneness which underpins all life. We have also seen how in different religious movements the vision of paradise is linked to the age-old desire to defeat death, to become a new self in a new heaven or a new earth. Just as the New Age followers embrace these ancient beliefs and desires, so they welcome Gaia.

Lovelock did not liken Gaia, or the earth, to paradise; the New Age belief that the earth has a consciousness seems at first to have little to do with the Persian *pairidaeza*. Yet the belief in Gaia returns us to some of the key themes which have long surrounded the subject of paradise: sexism, punishment and reward, gardens and enclosures.

The New Age emphasis on Gaia has brought the goddess to the fore at the expense of the male god of the Old Testament, and in keeping with the long-held view that Nature is as a feminine force. In turn, this has helped provide a forum for feminist thinkers to address the misogyny of the early creation myths such as Pandora's Jar (*see page 39*), and Adam's prior, superior creation over Eve. It rejects the male domination over women that these stories seem to countenance.

Some feminists argue that before the advent of patriarchal culture lies a paradise lost; others disagree, claiming that although there were goddesses, these were no more important than the gods.

In terms of ethics, many Gaia followers see the Earth Mother as a guardian of morality, who punishes and rewards humans for their actions. They believe that Gaia wishes to maintain internal harmony, but will dominate (and indeed obliterate) those who threaten it. For her followers, Gaia is Nature and the earth is her sacred body. From this perspective, it is important to experience the power of the goddess. Through divination, ritual, and magic Gaia followers participate in the energy of the goddess, helping the energy flow that will assist in the healing process and foster well-being.

In terms of Gaia, there can be no paradise unless we foster harmony with Nature and feel at one with her. In terms of enclosures, Gaia is a reminder that we live in a global culture. Gaia implies it is no longer sufficient to dream of an isolated protected haven on the earth in which the chosen can meet the divine and live in a state of spiritual bliss while the less fortunate wait

ABOVE: Photographs of the earth viewed from space have become a powerful modern symbol of harmony; Gaia followers see in them evidence of a global consciousness and proof that the planet is a unified system.

outside. For, in Gaia all things are interconnected and there are no insiders or outsiders. The garden has lost its boundaries.

Whatever we think of the scientific hypothesis or its New Age applications, Gaia serves as a powerful metaphor in a continuing debate about how humans should use the resources of the earth. If the entire earth is a garden, it can only be transformed back into a paradise by attention being given to the garden, the beings within the garden, and also the gardener.

The archetypal tale of the Garden of Eden also has a new relevance and meaning here: it recognizes the possibility of a new "Satan" who will lead us to a new Fall, but one that consists of planetary extinction rather than temporary exile. Perhaps we will find Satan in our global garden, perhaps we will find that Satan is the way that we cultivate the land. Given the pesticides and pollutants, the genetically modified crops and the threat of global warming, the challenge is chilling in its apocalyptic vision: inspect the orchard before you take a bite of the apple. You may be eating poisoned fruit.

GLOSSARY

A

Akh (plural Akhu) In Ancient Egyptian religion, the transfigured spirit of the blessed dead. Meaning "light," akh is closely associated with the journey of the sun.

Akkadian Earliest known Semitic language, spoken by the Assyrians and Babylonians, written in cuneiform (wedge-shaped) script on (mostly) clay tablets, of which large quantities have been preserved. The script was deciphered in the early nineteenth century.

Amitabha Also known as Amida in Japan, the Buddha of Measureless (or Infinite) Light. Often identified with Amitayus, the Buddha of Infinite Life. Amitabha is the personification of Compassion and the Buddha of the Pure Land (*q.v.*).

Apocrypha Word meaning hidden things that may refer either to a collection of writings associated with the Bible but excluded from the canon (*q.v.*) or, more particularly, to works accepted as divinely inspired in the Catholic and Orthodox traditions, but rejected by Protestants as uncanonical.

Arcadia Mountainous region in southern Greece, which was adopted by Virgil as the location of his pastoral *Eclogues* and has since come to stand for a life in the country dominated by the simple pleasures of song, dance, and courtship.

Ascension The bodily ascent of a human being into heaven, whether before death (e.g. Elijah) or after death (e.g. Jesus).

Avalon Blissful kingdom of the dead in Welsh mythology; then an earthly paradise in the western seas; later still the abode of heroes to which King Arthur was conveyed in his last battle; eventually identified with Glastonbury in Somerset.

B

Ba In Ancient Egyptian religion, the essence of a dead person as he/she appears after death. Birds were consistently associated with the ba. New Kingdom texts depict the ba as a bird with a human head.

Bodhisattva Also known as "Buddha of Compassion." Buddhist term for one who renounces nirvana until all humanity has ceased to suffer.

Book of the Dead Egyptian New Kingdom funerary text, properly named *The Book of Going Forth by Day*, collected from funerary equipment, coffins, and walls of burial chambers; attests to the weighing of souls by the god Osiris (*q.v.*).

Books of Hours Compilations of the psalms, readings, and prayers used in the Divine Office, divided into several "hours" (traditionally seven) and sung or recited daily by clerical members of monastic orders. They frequently contain illuminated illustrations of biblical and other scenes.

Buddha The title in Buddhism for one who is awakened and enlightened, who has become one with Supreme Truth.

Buraq In Islam, the magical beast on which the Prophet Mohammed ascends to heaven in the Mi'raj (*q.v.*).

C

Calypso In Greek mythology, Calypso is the divine island queen and sea-goddess who promised Odysseus (*q.v.*) immortality and eternal youth.

Canon Collection of writings accepted as authoritative by Jews or Christians, and together making up the Jewish and Christian Bibles.

Cherubim Winged celestial beings, entrusted in the Bible with several different tasks, such as guarding the way to the tree of life after the expulsion of Adam and Eve, and carrying the divine throne in the vision of Ezekiel 10.

Cockaigne Legendary land of plenty, in which food and drink was always freely available to everybody.

Coffin Texts Egyptian funerary texts of the Middle Kingdom, in part deriving from Old Kingdom *Pyramid Texts* (*q.v.*) and containing texts included in the New Kingdom *Book of the Dead* (*q.v.*). Features texts found on coffins and in burial chambers.

D

Daniel Biblical book, named after its protagonist, who is presented as having lived during the reign of the last kings of the neo-Babylonian Empire and their first successors, the early kings of the Medes and Persians, i.e., during most of the sixth century B.C.E.; although the book was certainly composed much later, probably shortly before the death of Antiochus IV Epiphanes in 164 B.C.E.

Dreaming or **Dreamtime** In Aboriginal culture, terms which refer to the mythical period of world creation and to the ancestors, who remain a source of spiritual power and continue to influence the affairs of this world.

Dystopia Word denoting a miserably unhappy place, coined in contrast to "utopia," (*q.v.*) once this had come to mean an ideally happy place.

E

Eleusis In the Greek region of Attica, the site of the Mysteries (*q.v.*) performed in honor of the goddess Demeter. In classical mythology, Demeter grieved at Eleusis for her missing daughter, Persephone.

Elysian Fields Blissful abode of the dead in Greek and Roman mythology, originally reserved for heroes and the otherwise eminent, subsequently for the good: sometimes called Elysium or Elysian Plain. Also known as "Isles of the Blessed."

Enoch Pre-historical biblical character, thought to have been assumed into heaven without dying, who lent his name to a number of apocryphal Old Testament writings, the first of which (1 Enoch) opens with The Book of Watchers (*q.v.*).

Ezekiel Biblical book, named after a sixth-century prophet, which records a large number of visions and prophecies, including the so-called throne vision in chapters 1 and 10, and the prophecy of the valley of the bones in chapter 37.

F

Field of Rushes Also known as Field of Reeds, Offerings, Hetep. The Ancient Egyptian paradise, characterized by cultivation, an abundance of nature, an absence of labor, and waterways.

G

Gaia To the Ancient Greeks, Gaia was the divine Earth Mother. In the 1960s, the scientist James Lovelock argued that the earth acts as a super-organism and called his scientific theory "Gaia."

Golden Age The lost mythical age of glory. The first of Hesiod's (*q.v.*) five ages of man, characterized by virtue, harmony, the abundance of nature, and absence of labor.

Gopis The young women with whom the Hindu God Krishna "dallied" as a young man. They became distraught with love, which came to symbolize the love of the soul for God.

H **Happy Hunting Ground** The Native American heaven, as described by the novelist James Fenimore Cooper in *The Last of the Mohicans*.

Harrowing of hell Term used of Christ's visit to Limbo (*q.v.*) immediately after his death to release the souls imprisoned there and enable them to enter paradise.

Hephaestus (Vulcan to the Romans) The Greek god of fire and worker of metals, expelled from Mount Olympus (*q.v.*). Creator of the first woman, Pandora (*q.v.*).

Heracles Hero of classical myth, known for his great strength. He successfully completed twelve labors, including taking the golden apples from the Garden of the Hesperides (*q.v.*) and joined the gods on Mount Olympus (*q.v.*) after his death.

Hesiod Early Greek poet, dates uncertain, whose works *Theogony* and *Works and Days* were put into writing in the eighth century B.C.E.

Hesperides, Garden of the Site of tree with golden apples, guarded by the serpent Ladon (often depicted as a dragon) and the three nymph sisters, the Hesperides.

Hieroglyph In Ancient Egypian writing, a figure of an object (tree, animal, etc.) representing a word or sound. Found on monuments and records in burial sites.

Holy of Holies The innermost sanctuary (debir) of the Jerusalem Temple, which housed the Ark of the Covenant, and which nobody was allowed to enter, with the exception of the high priest on the Day of Atonement.

Homer Early Greek poet, of uncertain dates, whose work was put into writing in the eighth century B.C.E. Author of *The Iliad* and *The Odyssey*. He has often been regarded as the father of Western poetry.

I **Ichan Tonatiuh Ilhuijcan** Aztec heaven or "house of the sun," in which the blessed dead lived in service to the sun for a period of four years before being transformed into birds or butterflies.

L **Last Judgment** In Christian teaching, the day of final reckoning at the end of time, when all mankind will be judged according to its merits.

Levi One of the twelve sons of Jacob, patriarchal ancestor of the tribe that bears his name, and credited with the authorship of the apocryphal and largely Christian *Testament of Levi*.

Limbo Term meaning fringe or border that refers to the state or place of those souls who did not deserve the punishments of hell but could not enter heaven until Christ, by his death and resurrection, had earned their redemption.

M **Mag Mell** The Happy Plain or Plain of Happiness, the paradise island of Celtic mythology.

Mahayana Branch of Buddhism known as the Great Vehicle. Generally Mahayana acknowledges human limitations and encompasses Pure Land (*q.v.*) teachings.

Mandala A diagram used by Buddhists to aid meditation.

Marco Polo Thirteenth-century Venetian merchant and voyager, whose *Travels* include reports of Prester John (*q.v.*) and the Old Man of the Mountain (*q.v.*).

Merkabah Hebrew word meaning "chariot" which is applied to one of the two main Jewish mystical traditions based on the prophecies in Ezekiel 1 and 10.

Michael One of the leading angels (archangels) in Jewish and Christian tradition, regularly portrayed as the leader of the forces of God against those of the devil. His name means: Who resembles God?

Mictlan The underworld of Aztec religion, presided over by the god Mictlantecuhtli, destiny for mortals who led undistinguished lives.

Mir'aj In Islam, the Prophet Mohammed's ascension to heaven, in which the Prophet, guided by the angel Gabriel, visits the seven heavens.

Mishnah A collection of tractates (studies and commentaries) upon the Oral Law that was believed to have been handed down from Moses, published around 200 C.E., and forming the basis of all subsequent legal teaching in Judaism.

Mount Meru In Hinduism, the mythical golden mountain at the center of the world.

Mount Olympus The abode of the gods of Ancient Greece, where Zeus (*q.v.*) reigned supreme. Located at the summit of the mountain, the home of the gods was out of reach to mortals.

Mysteries Ancient Greek rituals in which knowledge of secret and esoteric truths ensured an afterlife of prosperous ease. The Mysteries were later adopted and adapted by the Romans.

N **Nebuchadnezzar** King of Babylon, 605–562 B.C.E., who figures prominently (and anachronistically) in the Book of Daniel (*q.v.*).

Neoplatonism A philosophical school founded by Plotinus in the third century C.E., offering a novel interpretation of the teachings of Plato, and exerting a strong influence on contemporary Christian theologians.

Nirvana Buddhist term referring to the "extinction" or "blowing out" of the self and release from the limitations of existence, the spiritual goal of Buddhism.

O **Odysseus** Hero of Homer's *Odyssey*, the epic poem which records his mythical adventures and various encounters with the Greek gods on the homeward journey from Troy.

Old Man of the Mountain Character in the *Travels* of Marco Polo (*q.v.*) who is said to have constructed a garden paradise imitating the paradise of the Quran.

Osiris Egyptian god who became increasingly associated with the sun. Murdered by his brother Seth, Osiris was a resurrected god. In *The Book of the Dead*, he is responsible for the judgment of the dead.

P **Pairidaeza** Persian origin of the word paradise, from *pairi* (around) and *daeza* (wall); a walled enclosure. "Pairidaeza" described the Persian royal park enclosures.

Pandora In Greek mythology, the first woman. Her name literally means "all-gifted." According to Hesiod (*q.v.*), she was created by Hephaestus (*q.v.*) on Zeus' (*q.v.*) orders, as a punishment to man. "Pandora's Box" is a phrase referring to a gift that appears desirable but is in fact a curse.

Pardes Hebrew loan-word from the Greek *paradeisos*, referring in biblical usage to a garden or orchard, and then later in the teaching of the rabbis to the heavenly paradise.

Pharisees Jewish sect, first emerging as an organized body around 140 B.C.E., the spiritual ancestors of rabbinical Judaism, and among the first Jews to profess the doctrine of the resurrection (*q.v.*).

Prester John Legendary priest and potentate, believed (because of a spurious letter circulated in his name) to have ruled over a vast kingdom in Asia during the twelfth century.

Procopius Byzantine Greek historian, (c.500–565 C.E.), secretary to Belisarius (the Emperor Justinian's leading general) and author of an eight-volume history of Justinian's wars, including those against the Goths.

Prometheus A Titan (*q.v.*) in Greek mythology. The giver of fire to mankind, an act for which he was severely punished and which led to the creation of the first woman, Pandora (*q.v.*).

Pure Land The western paradise of the Pure Land school of Mahayana (*q.v.*) Buddhism, from which nirvana (*q.v.*) will be attained with certainty and ease.

Pyramid Texts Old Kingdom funerary texts of Ancient Egypt, consisting of written spells carved on the tomb walls of royal pyramids.

Q Quran The sacred scripture of Muslims, the Word of God, revealed to the Prophet Mohammed by the angel Gabriel in the seventh century C.E.

R Ra Egyptian word for "sun." Ra is the Ancient Egyptian creation god who journeys in the solar barque (*q.v.*). The fortunate (such as deceased kings) merge with Ra after death or live alongside him as akhu (*q.v.*).

Resurrection (of the body). Doctrine taught by certain Jews and all early Christians asserting that believers will rise bodily from the dead at the Last Judgment (*q.v.*).

S Sanhedrin Hebraized form of the Greek *synedrion*, "sitting-together," "session." The Sanhedrin was the supreme political, religious, and judicial body of the Jews during the period of the Roman rule of Palestine, both before and after the destruction of the Temple in 70 C.E.

Shangri-La The paradisaical Buddhist monastery in *Lost Horizon* by James Hilton that subsequently came to symbolize any remote or unattainable place of blissful happiness.

Síd (Sídh). One of numerous Celtic hills or mounds, each thought of as occupied by one of the gods and as the door to an underground realm of inexhaustible splendor and light.

Solar barque In Ancient Egyptian religion, the boat in which the sun god crosses the sky and journeys through the underworld.

T Talmud One of two (Babylonian/Palestinian) collections of Jewish teaching, containing extensive elaborations and interpretations of the Mishnah (*q.v.*), composed over nearly three centuries and completed toward the end of the fifth century C.E.

Theravada Branch of Buddhism once known as Hinayana, "the lesser wheel" of salvation, but now as the Way of the Elders.

Titans In Greek mythology, primordial beings of great strength, typically brutish and lawless. Atlas, the gardener of the orchard containing the apples of the Hesperides (*q.v.*) was a Titan.

Tlalocan The Aztec paradise of the east, presided over by the rain god, Tlaloc. A place of permanent springtime and eternal abundance.

Troubadours Wandering minstrels, lyric poets of chivalric love, who flourished in Provence, southern France, from the eleventh to the thirteenth century C.E.

Tuatha Dé Danaan Collective name of the gods of the ancient Celts (literally "the folk of the god whose mother is Dana"), originally regarded as powers of light and knowledge, but subsequently relegated by Christianity to the rank of fairies or identified with the fallen angels.

Typology Christian practice of interpreting events, characters, and places in the Old Testament as intentionally anticipating or foreshadowing events, etc. in the New.

Tyre Proverbially wealthy merchant city on the coast of Phoenicia (modern Lebanon), whose king figures as a rival to God in the prophecy of Ezekiel (chapters 26–28).

U Uruk A large walled city in ancient Mesopotamia, which according to Babylonian tradition was ruled over by Gilgamesh.

Utopia A word that originally meant "nowhere" but which came to mean an ideal world, the imagined realization of unattainable longings.

V Valhalla "Hall of the Slain": in Norse mythology the palatial heavenly home of dead warriors, to which they were welcomed by the god Odin.

Valkyries "Choosers of the Slain": supernatural female beings, riding through the air in the service of Odin, who required them to determine the course of human battles, and then to wait upon the fallen warriors in Valhalla (*q.v.*).

Virgil Poet of Ancient Rome, 70–19 B.C.E., best known for the *Aeneid* and *Eclogues*. His poetry articulated the idea of the Golden Age (*q.v.*) and romanticized Arcadia (*q.v.*) as a place of pastoral beauty.

Vulgate Latin translation of the Christian Bible, largely attributable to Saint Jerome, who in 389 C.E. embarked on a new version that soon came to be regarded as authoritative in the Roman church.

W Watchers Name of the rebel angels in The Book of Watchers (1 Enoch 1–36).

Y Yggdrasil Mighty ash, the world-tree, thought in Norse mythology to mark the center of the universe.

Yuga An age or period of time in Hindu chronology. There are four world ages; the first is krita, an age of virtue, harmony, happiness, and righteousness.

Z Zeus The supreme god of Greek mythology (Roman equivalent is Jupiter). Ultimately responsible for all that happens on heaven and earth, associated with lightning and the eagle, symbols of his power.

INDEX

BIBLIOGRAPHY

Barr, James, *The Garden of Eden and the Hope of Immortality*, SCM Press, London 1992

Blair, Emma Helen (ed.), *Indian Tribes of the Upper Mississipi Valley and Regions of the Great Lakes*, Arthur H. Clark Company, USA 1911

Blair, S. S., Bloom, J. M. (eds.), *Images of Paradise in Islamic Art*, Museum of Art, Dartmouth College, USA 1991

Brock, Sebastian (trans.), *Ephraem's Hymns on Paradise*, St Vladimir's Seminary Press, USA 1990

Brooke, Rupert, *Poetical Works*, Faber & Faber, London 1970

Caruana, Wally, *Aboriginal Art*, Thames and Hudson, London 1993

Carey, John (ed.), *Faber Book of Utopias*, Faber & Faber, London 1999

Charlesworth, James H. (ed.), *Old Testament Pseudepigrapha*, Vol 1, Doubleday, UK 1983

Charlesworth, Morphy, Bell, and Maddock (eds.), *Religion in Aboriginal Australia*, University of Queensland Press, Australia 1984

Clark, Emma, *Underneath Which Rivers Flow: the Symbolism of the Islamic Garden*, Prince of Wales Institute of Architecture, UK 1996

Fitzgerald, F. Scott, *The Great Gatsby*, Penguin, London 1969

Haleem, Muhammad Abdel, *Understanding the Quran*, Tauris, London 1999

Herbert, Zbigniew, *Selected Poems*, Milosz, Czeslaw and Scott, Peter Dale (trans.), Carcanet Press , UK 1985

Hesiod, *Theogony/Works and Days*, West M.L. (trans.), OUP, UK 1988

Homer, *The Iliad*, Fagles, Robert (trans.), Penguin, London 1990

Homer, *The Odyssey*, Fagles, Robert (trans.), Penguin, London 1990

Horace, *The Odes and the Epodes*, Bennett, C. E. (trans.), Cambridge, Massachusetts 1946

Hultkrantz, Åke, *Belief and Worship in Native North America*, Syracuse University Press 1981

Lewis, R. W. B., *The American Adam*, Chicago 1955

Lovelock, J.E. *Gaia, a New Look at Life on Earth*, OUP, UK 1979

McDannell, Colleen and Lang, Bernhard, *Heaven: A History*, Yale University Press, New Haven/New York 1988

Milton, John, *Paradise Lost*, Longman, UK 1968

Morey-Gaines, Ann-Janine, *Apples and Ashes, Culture, Metaphor, and Morality in the American Dream*, American Academy of Religion Academy Series, 1982

Morphy, Howard, *Aboriginal Art*, Phaidon Press, London 1998

O'Reilly, Jennifer, "The Trees of Eden in Mediaeval Iconography," in *A Walk in the Garden: Biblical, Topographical and Literary Images of Eden*, Morris, P. and Sawyer, D. (eds.), Sheffield Academic Press, UK 1992

Ovid, *Metamorphoses I–IV* (Classical Texts), Hill, D. E. (trans.), Aris and Phillips, UK 1985

Ray, Benjamin C., *African Religions, Symbol, Ritual and Community*, Prentice-Hall, UK 1976

Rumi's Divan of Shems of Tabriz, Cowan, J. (trans.), Element, UK 1997

Speck, Frank, *Naskapi*, University of Oklahoma Press 1935

Sundkler, Bengt, *Zulu Zion and some Swazi Zionists*, OUP, UK 1976

The Bible, Authorized King James Version, 1611

The Quran, *The Meaning of The Glorious Quran*, Text and Explanatory Translation by Marmaduke Pickthall (Vols. 1 and 2), published by Hyperabad-Deccan, Government Central Press, India 1938

Thwaites, Reuben Gold (ed.), *Jesuit Relations and Allied Documents 1896-1901*, 73 Vols., Rowman and Littlefield, Ohio 1959

Walker, Benjamin, *Hindu World: An Encyclopedic Survey of Hinduism* (2 Vols.), Allen & Unwin, London 1961

Wasson, Robert Gordon, *The Road to Eleusis*, Harcourt, Brace, Jovanovich, USA 1978

Yeats, W. B., *Collected Poems*, Finneran, R. J. (ed.), Macmillan, UK 1933

ACKNOWLEDGMENTS

The authors and Quarto would like to acknowledge and thank the following copyright holders for permission to quote text:

Page 33: Hesiod, *Theogony/Works and Days*, © M.L. West 1988, by permission of Oxford University Press; 36: "The Rage of Achilles" by Homer, from *The Iliad* by Homer, translated by Robert Fagles, copyright © 1990 by Robert Fagles. Introduction and Notes Copyright © 1990 by Bernard Knox. Used by permission of Viking Penguin, a division of Penguin Putnam Inc; 36 & 41: From *The Odyssey* by Homer, translated by Robert Fagles, copyright © 1996 by Robert Fagles. Used by permission of Viking Penguin, a division of Penguin Putnam Inc; 42: *The Road to Eleusis* by Robert Gordon Wasson © William Dailey Rare Books; 65: The Syballine Oracles Book V, from *Old Testament Psuedepigrapha* Vol 1, James H. Charlesworth (ed.), Doubleday 1983 © Random House Inc;

99: *Rumi's Divan of Shems of Tabriz*, translation copyright © James Cowan; 122: W. B. Yeats, *Sailing to Byzantium*, A. P. Watt Ltd on behalf of Michael B. Yeats, and reprinted with the permission of Scribner, a Division of Simon & Schuster, Inc., from *The Collected Poems of W. B. Yeats*: Revised 2nd Edition by Richard J. Fenneran. Copyright © 1928 by Macmillan Publishing Co. copyright renewed © 1956 by Georgie Yeats; 136: "Report from Paradise" from *Zbigniew Herbert: Selected Poems*, p. 131, translated by Czeslaw Milosz and Peter Dale Scott (Penguin Books 1968), translation © Czeslaw Milosz and Peter Dale Scott, 1968; 145: *Zulu Zion and some Swazi Zionists* by Bengt Sundkler by permission of Oxford University Press.

John Ashton would like to thank Dr Jeremy Black of the Oriental Institute, Oxford, for his assistance with the chapter on Sumer; Dr Sebastian Brock of the same Institute for permission to reproduce his translation of Ephraem; his friend and collaborator Tom Whyte for many useful suggestions; and editor Tracie Lee for her patience and general helpfulness. Tom Whyte would like to thank John Ashton, John Mackessy, Simone Ling, Clare Palmer, Wendy Katz, Sharon Holm, Sarah Lush, Stan Hawthorne, Natalie Man, Lawrence Santcross, Neil Hudson, Louis Brenner, Charlie Gore, Doug Osto, Louisa Young, Hans Brill, Francesca Brill, and Rebecca Lily Bowen.